Assets on Blockchain

Security Token Offerings and the tokenization of securities

Max Kops

Copyright © 2019 Max Kops
All rights reserved.

Disclaimer
The information in this book shall provide helpful information and input on the topic of security token offerings. The author only shares what he has learned from thorough research, experience from past and present activities and last but not least personal perception. The content of the book represents the opinion of the author and although the content has been prepared using best efforts, it cannot be assured that all information is correct, especially since in this fast-moving field, updates and changes follow quickly. The validity of any statement cannot be guaranteed at a later point in time after the release of the book.

This book is not meant to provide legal, financial or another professional services advice. For this kind of advice, consult a professional before making decisions for your business.

The publisher and author make no representations or warranties and assume no liabilities of any kind regarding the accuracy or completeness of the content of this book. They specifically disclaim any implied warranties of merchantability or fitness of use for any particular purpose. Neither the author nor the publisher shall be held liable or responsible to any person or entity regarding any loss or incidental or consequential damages caused, or alleged to have been caused, directly or indirectly, by the information contained in this book. No warranty may be created or extended by sales representatives or written sales materials.

All references provided are only for informational purposes and do not constitute endorsement of the sources' authors. Readers should be aware that any information on the internet can be subject to change.

Table of Contents

About the Author vii

Preface: The disruption of the financial industry ix

Introductory: Getting started with the Blockchain 1
    What is a Blockchain? 2
    What are distributed ledger technologies? 7
    Terminologies: Tokens, Coins, Currencies 10

Tokenization 15
    How tokens become assets 15
    The advantages of tokens 17
    The disadvantages of tokens 22

Case Study: Tokenization of Real Estate 25

Initial Coin Offerings and Security Token Offerings 33
    Initial Coin Offerings (ICOs): Raising money by selling tokens .. 33
    The ICO wild west: How ICOs escaped the Regulation 38
    Case Study: The difference between ICOs and STOs 43

Table of Contents

What are Security Token Offerings? 45

When to STO and when not to STO 49

Security Token Offerings in detail 53
    The stakeholders in a STO 53
    Security Token Exchanges / Secondary Markets 55
    Custody 56
    KYC and AML 56
    STO vs. IPO 59
    Facts & Figures 61

The Process of Security Token Offerings (STOs) 65
    1. Defining the business model 66
    2. Defining the token use-case (ICO)
    or the token structure (STO) 68
    3. Defining the stages of Fundraising 77
    4. Defining the target investor group 80
    5. Adjusting the documents for investors 87
    6. Dealing with secondary markets 87
    7. Setting up the Banking & Finance infrastructure 89
    8. Choosing the issuing platform 90
    9. Reaching out to Pre-STO investors 91

Table of Contents

    10. Choosing the type of token **91**

    11. Preparing the legal setup for the Pre-STO round(s) **92**

    12. Running the Pre-STO rounds **93**

    13. Redefining the STO strategy **94**

    14. Preparing the technical setup for a public tokensale **95**

    15. Integrating Know-Your-Customer and Anti-Money-Laundering processes **98**

    16. Auditing the technical infrastructure **98**

    17. Running the public tokensale **99**

    18. Post-STO work and managing the money **100**

Blockchain Platforms for tokenization **103**

    General considerations **103**

    Different Blockchain Platforms in comparison **105**

Token Standards **113**

    The requirements of an asset-backed token **114**

    Token Standardization **115**

    Standards specifically for security tokens on Ethereum **120**

    Summary: Security Token Standards **123**

Regulation of Security Token Offerings (STOs) **125**

    Regulations within the European Union **138**

Table of Contents

Is the Whitepaper a prospectus? **149**

Exemptions **151**

STOs within the European Union **153**

STOs in Asia **160**

Regulation in South America **166**

Regulations in the United States **168**

Regulation in Australia **172**

Summary **173**

Book Summary... **175**

Closing words **177**

The exclusive readers' portal.. **178**

About the Author

Max Kops is a Blockchain Thought Leader and a bestselling author. While having been programming from an early age, he started to mine Bitcoins in the bedroom of his father as a teenager. Soon he realized the true potential of Blockchain technologies and started to produce content for his own blog and leading international magazines.

During the time he graduated in Information Systems and led the IT department of a student consultancy, he quickly understood that groundbreaking technologies have to be made applicable and accessible for the business world. He started analyzing Blockchain companies and evaluated more than 1,000 startups for subscribers. Seeing the good and the bad companies, he understood that many companies had an excellent business model but were lacking the capacity and competence in conducting an Initial Coin Offering (ICO). Max quit his job as an Analyst and then helped ICOs to be successful by providing him the perspective he had gained on 1,000 projects. Since then, he got invited as a speaker to the most-relevant Blockchain conferences in Europe and further travelled to Asia.

His mission with the *Assets on Blockchain* program is to bring knowledge about tokenization and the disruption of the existing financial space into the world.

Max is writing on his blog at maxkops.com

Preface: The disruption of the financial industry

The financial system is huge and somehow like a cruise ship: It carries a lot, has a high responsibility and changing the direction can take a long time. However, within the last two years, terms surrounding the *Blockchain* topic more and more came up to the mainstream and *security tokens*, *token offerings* and *Blockchain based transactions* are being discussed as the disruptor of the financial system. The technology is new, the expectations are high and there is a lot of misinformation to be found everywhere. Will the Blockchain disrupt the financial system and enable companies to raise capital without the intervention of the bank? Will the financial ecosystem we know from the past soon be shrinked to a few smaller players, destroying the big banks in the game?

This book takes people interested in financial applications of the Blockchain, startups and people from the traditional financial ecosystem to the point of understanding the potential of Blockchain based assets and so-called *tokenization*. It conveys the process of a Security Token Offering (STO) in order to e.g. give out shares of a company to raise money for the startup. At the same time, it explains the new phenomenon of tokens for people

Preface: The disruption of the financial industry

from the financial industry. If you do not know yet what a token is, how it liberates the market and revolutionizes the settlement of financial transactions, you will learn all of that from the very beginning. **And if you are a startup, this book should convey the pros and cons of raising capital through a tokensale.**

While touching the surface of the technological elements, the book will deeply dive into Security Token Offerings from a combined tech-business view as well as it covers the Regulations worldwide concerning security tokens.

What you will learn in this book:
1. What a Blockchain is and why it is so relevant for the financial industry

2. Are Security Token Offerings (STOs) a relevant capital raisinng option for me and my company?

3. Why we should tokenize assets and how individuals and companies benefit of digital assets and shares

4. The upsides and downsides of tokenization

5. How STOs are conducted

6. What is the standpoint of regulators worldwide towards tokenized assets? Which governments support DLT based technologies and which step away?

6. The impact on the financial industry and on classical Initial Public Offerings (IPOs) on stock exchanges?

Preface: The disruption of the financial industry

This book is the right choice for you, when:
1) You heard of "Blockchain", "Tokens", "ICOs" or "cryptocurrencies" and want to understand the motives behind as well as how digital assets work

2) You are a startup and you want to evaluate the STO as a funding vehicle

3) You want to learn how tokens provide new access to asset classes and liberate certain markets

4) You expect a hands-on guide and a practically written book

This book is not the right choice for you, when:
1) You want to dive into the technical details of general Blockchain technologies or want to learn programming

2) You want to invest in cryptocurrencies and look for advice

3) You expect academic research

The content of this book

After highlighting different use-cases of Blockchains and distributed ledgers, such as tokenizing your existing assets for higher liquidity, fundraising money through the Blockchain and using decentralized currencies, the book will explain the aspects of a STO and propose **the first standard process for conducting an offering of tokenized assets ever.** This should enlighten the nowadays still intransparent and often disorganized process of performing a fundraising with the help of tokens. If you are working in the financial industry or you are advising clients in

Preface: The disruption of the financial industry

that area, you will also be able to evaluate whether the new technological opportunities are a) relevant for your business b) a use-case for expanding your business or c) which disruptions could affect your business.

If you are a startup or someone managing any form of value (such as asset managers or family offices), you will understand what tokenization means for your purpose to be applied as well as which opportunities such offer as an asset class.

The book will go in hand with some bonus material published on my website. Since the technology and the ecosystem is evolving rapidly, statistics and numbers can be outdated within a couple of weeks. By using the links, you can check the latest updates of the statistics I am providing online.

The aim of this book is to make the topic tangible for everybody – whether one has a legal, technical, any other background or is a student in highschool. And it should get people started. This is why I decided to talk to you directly – your lifetime is too valuable to make things complicated.

Let's get tokenized.

Another note: For the purpose of transmitting general knowledge about security tokens and tokenization, it is kept it as objective as I could. Therefore, no specific providers are mentioned or recommended. The reason for not mentioning possible providers here is not only that it could cause a conflict of interest, but also the fact that in the time-being there are no *"one fits all"* solutions yet that I would feel comfortable in recommending at any given

Preface: The disruption of the financial industry

case. Pointing out the right partners to work with, fluently implementing the strategy and not being overcharged are some of the services I offer as a consultant but can impossibly cover within this book.

Many people showed their interested in receiving information about specific platforms, providers and services that can be used to conduct a STO. Therefore, the exclusive web portal for the readers of this book serves the purpose of enriching the facts presented in this book with specific use-cases, providers, services and platforms. I am a partner of some of them and feel comfortable in recommending. You can access the web portal with the code given below.

The exclusive readers portal for this book
Everybody who has bought this book can obtain access to the exclusive web portal. Since a book is printed once with the information given at the time of writing, specifics can be outdated quickly and the time for publishing a renewed version of the book cannot keep up with the technological advancements.

The web portal aims to provide updated information and interesting news at the best possible frequency. Subscribe to the newsletter, so you automatically receive updates and do not miss important changes and information in the field of security tokens.

How can I find the portal?
    The portal is available at:
    assetsonblockchain.com/booklounge

Preface: The disruption of the financial industry

You can register your account by using the code:
20aob19

Preface: The disruption of the financial industry

Is there a fee attached to the portal?
Accessing the portal is forever free with the above-mentioned code. We will try to keep the the portal up as long as possible to provide you with the most-relevant and groundbreaking updates in the sphere of Security Token Offerings and Tokenization.

Link codes used in this book
In order to make the access to further resources as easy as possible, a link code website is provided. Whenever you see a link code mentioned in the text, you can type it in here:

assetsonblockchain.com/link

These links will lead you directly to the additional material and you can save the time of manually typing this link into your browser.

Introductory: Getting started with the Blockchain

It was 2008 when the worlds' population finally realized the inevitable. The financial crisis has officially begun. The economy went worse and people lost their faith into banks. At the same time, and probably for the same reason, the Bitcoin was invented. A currency that survives without any government and without any bank. Distributed around the world so there are no single point of failures and attacking the system is difficult – following mottos like *code is the law* and the *people own it*.

The stone was set for the evolution of what we call a Blockchain today – the technology that enabled the Bitcoin to be invented. And what started with just a currency is now enabling humans to digitize their assets – again: without a bank. Instead of having the digital assets managed by a bank, they are stored on a distributed database, secured by mathematical algorithms and replicated worldwide. No single point of failure, no oligopoly over the financial system.

In the following, we will start from the very basics of what a Blockchain is, how cryptocurrencies work and move over to the

Introductory: Getting started with the Blockchain

actual topic of tokens that enable us to digitize assets on the Blockchain.

What is a Blockchain?

Asking what a Blockchain is, it makes sense to start with an explanation of classical databases and raise the question why we need a new paradigm for storing data since storing information is nothing new.

Whenever data is generated on platforms like social media, it is saved into a database that belongs to the owner. Every click we do, every friendship we have or every message we send for example on Facebook is stored in a database that Facebook owns.

The same principle is used when banking transactions are made: You simply send a request to your bank telling it that you wish to transfer money to person X. The bank then starts the process of subtracting the respective amount of money from your account and adding it to the other account. It has a database somewhere in which the balance of every customer is saved. When a transaction happens, the bank just updates the information about who possesses how much money in the respective database. Since we trust in the bank acting upon our will, the operation lies onto them. We hand in our order *"Please transfer this amount of money to X"* and the bank does that for us.

Why a Blockchain?

The Blockchain comes into place when we imagine transactions <u>without</u> banks – or even without any intermediaries. How is it possible that there is no bank that ensures everybody has access

Introductory: Getting started with the Blockchain

to the money he or she really possesses? What if people claim that they possess more money than they actually do and there is no central database that stores this information and a bank that operates it?

Bitcoin was the first application of a Blockchain and brought exactly that into practice – giving the users a monetary system that they can run by themselves, without a third-party intermediary like a bank. This is the first principle of a Blockchain: **decentralization**. The network is not run by a single intermediary like the bank, instead many different people run it on their own. In the case of Bitcoin that means many people offer their computing power to the network to perform calculations and keep up the operation of it – so-called *miners*. The bank hence gets replaced by a number of unknown people that now take care of transactions being processed correctly. If a bank is doing that, we trust the bank with its name, the registered entity and the banking license it has. In the case of cryptocurrencies, the same work is done by stranger individuals (the *miners*) online that do not even need to reveal their identity. Simply speaking, you do not know the persons who are responsible for executing your transfer of money and still need to trust them – hence, the Blockchain implements certain measures to ensure everybody who participates in running the system acts faithfully and that the transactions can be validated. This is absolutely necessary in order to have a decentralized network of many unknown participants.

The second principle is **distribution**. Not only is the Blockchain administrated by many different parties, the *data* itself is also duplicated at many different places. Therefore, it is difficult to

Introductory: Getting started with the Blockchain

attack the system since the nodes and the miners are distributed worldwide. *Miners* are processig the trasactions and *nodes* are responsible for validating the information and storing the Blockchain, however, these distinctions are not relevant for the purpose of this book. Imagine a bank with their executives and their physical offices – stopping the operation of that bank would be easy. If a network consists of millions of operators, we can fairly call it resistant against governmental or regulatory interference.

The explanation above refers to the key principles of a Blockchain that were invented in 2008. There are many more specifications, for example a Blockchain does not necessarily need to be open for everybody to participate. So called *private* Blockchains only allow certain, selected and identified parties to operate. This is an necessary aspect – financial transactions for example require identification, certainty and stability of the operators.

The third, often referred, element of a Blockchain is **transparency**. Depending on the type of Blockchain (public or private) it is possible that every transaction is visible for everybody. A private Blockchain does not reveal this information to everybody, but only to a small network of participants that are manually selected. In this case, it is still transparent because every action that is performed on the data is being recorded. If anybody acts unfaithful, the other parties could detect it. An example would be a consortium of five different banks that share one Blockchain. They do not want anyone outside of the consortium to see the information, so they would use a private Blockchain. However, if transactions between the banks are made, they can see the transactions and bank 1 could detect a fraudulent activity that bank 2 did to hurt bank 3.

Introductory: Getting started with the Blockchain

Security might be a blurry term, however Blockchains are often called secure since they are based on mathematical procedures and hash functions, making them *immutable*. If someone wants to manipulate the data contained in a Blockchain, such an attempt would be detected by using the mathematical functions for verifying the information. If a person tried to cheat, everybody else would immediately notice that. The same goes for editing or erasing existing data: Since everybody has a copy of the last state of the Blockchain, they would automatically notice if someone has changed or deleted some data. What is saved on to the Blockchain stays on the Blockchain.

A Blockchain is useful when there is no trust within the interaction of differet parties: If bank A and bank B would interact with each other and bank B is operating the database, then bank A would need to trust the other bank that it always enters the data correctly. This is simply not a good setting, so a Blockchain removes this trust issue. The database is neither owned by A, nor by B. Both of them can suggest that an entry in this distributed ledger is made, but only if both agree and form a consensus, the action is actually performed. Nobody has to rely on the other party, and everything is executed only upon the consent of both parties.

Summarizing the key elements of a Blockchain:

A) Decentralization: The network is operated by different parties and not owned by one central intermediary

B) Distribution: The data is replicated at different places

C) Transparency: Every action within the network is tracked and can be verified

Introductory: Getting started with the Blockchain

D) Security and immutability: Operations are based on mathematical functions and data can never be deleted

A Blockchain is a distributed ledger that is shared by certain parties (either openly or by selected parties) to create a trustworthy environment in which activities are monitored and data is stored without having to rely on one single entity or individual.

Why is it called a Blockchain?
A classical database as we know it for centuries can be imagined like this picture as one information following the other, row by row.

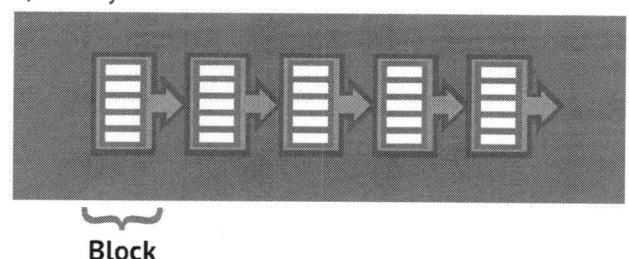

Block

On the other hand, in a Blockchain the information is stored in *blocks*. Many rows of data are put together into one block. Important is that the blocks themselves are connected to each other, literally a *chain* of *blocks* and therefore a *Blockchain*. Without diving too deep into the technological details, this structure enables the Blockchain to be secure against manipulation: the blocks are connected to each other and if you change any of the data within the blocks, they are losing the connection to the other blocks. This would be recognized by the users since they see the chain has changed and someone tried to perform a manipulation. All this is ensured by mathematical algorithms.

Introductory: Getting started with the Blockchain

As we spoke about transactions here, Blockchains have different use cases. Bitcoin is used for cryptocurrencies while Ethereum is used for so-called Smart Contracts and hundreds of other Blockchains have a different purpose.

What are distributed ledger technologies?

As explained above, a Blockchain consists of blocks. A *distributed ledger* on the other hand is a more abstract type of a system with the elements of the Blockchain, but not ordered in blocks. Therefore, a distributed ledger can also be distributed and decentralized, but ordered in a *tangle* (not relevant here) instead of connected *blocks*. For the purpose of this book, the distinction is not necessary. The short description shall only help you understand the term distributed ledger as an upper category when it is used in other resources.

The Blockchain is *one* type of a distributed ledger.

Summary: Blockchain and its context as a technology are following certain concepts such as decentralization, distribution and transparency.

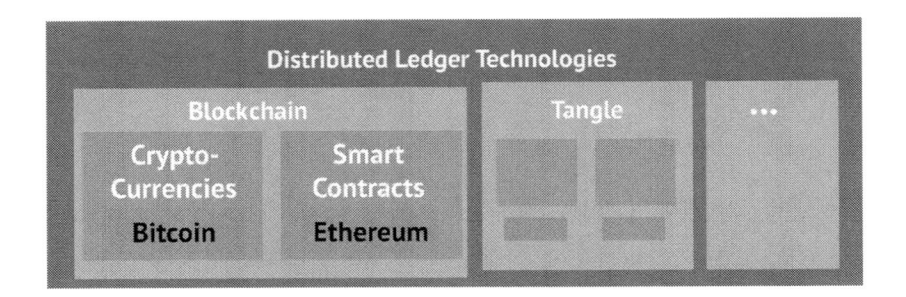

Distributed Ledger Technologies			
Blockchain		Tangle	...
Crypto-Currencies	Smart Contracts		
Bitcoin	Ethereum		

Introductory: Getting started with the Blockchain

A simple example to understand the trust issue the Blockchain solves

First hearing about the *Blockchain* or *distributed ledgers* might make people wonder why we need a complex, decentralized infrastructure if the databases and technologies we already know have been established over centuries. Inserting data row by row as we know it from computer sheets seems much easier.

This question is more than valid since Blockchains are unfortunately often used when they do not have any advantage compared to a classical, centralized database. This is actually much cost-heavier and a waste of resources. However, in many cases the Blockchain does add a lot of value or solely enables certain interactions or businesses to happen because of the decentralized nature.

In the following example, we will use the synonyms **Alice** and **Bob** that want to perform a car trade. Alice wants to sell her car and Bob is interested in buying it. They found each other on a digital car marketplace and unfortunately live very far from each other. Bob is fine with paying the premium for delivery into his city. However, he would need to pay Alice first without ever seeing if she really possesses the car. He could possibly give the money to the driver who will pick up the car. However, this driver cannot check if he received the right car. In this case, Bob could get scammed by Alice. Vice versa, Alice does not want to send the car to Bob without having received the payment before.

Together, Alice and Bob are stuck until one party volunteers to take the risk and pay the money or send the car first. This is the **trust issue** that exists between Alice and Bob.

Introductory: Getting started with the Blockchain

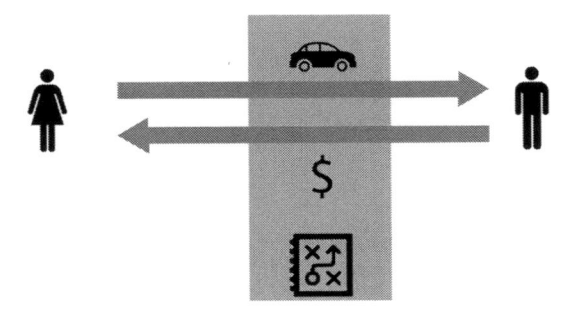

Now a *smart contract* could solve this problem. A Smart Contract is nothing else than an *if-else* construct. **If** a certain *condition* is met, **then** another *action* is performed. You can imagine the Smart Contract as a digital form of a notary sitting between two or more parties and ensuring that all of them act in a legal way according to the deal. In this case, the Smart Contract would work the following way:

1. Both Alice *and* Bob send their resources (the money and the car) to the Smart Contract

2. The Smart Contract constantly checks *"Have both parties performed their duty?"* If (**condition**) both parties did so, then (**action**) it hands over the car to Bob and the money to Alice.

In this case, the Smart Contract functions as an *escrow*. He holds the objects until both parties fulfilled all their duties and the action can be taken The difference to a notary who provides an escrow service is that no human intervention is needed. The notary as an intermediary gets replaced by a Smart Contract that executes the work he would usually do in an automated way. It will take some time till the transfer of physical goods can also be automated with a trustless transaction on the Blockchain – at the moment, it mostly works for digital processes.

Now, an escrow is just one application of Smart Contracts. The Smart Contract logic can be very complex to include many factors, information sources and decision trees. It can solve trust issues by programming legal contracts in a digital form and require a consensus to be reached in order to perform actions.

Three examples of Smart Contracts in real life

Flight delay: The Smart Contract constantly checks whether a flight was delayed (**condition**). If so, it refunds the ticket (**action**).

Company Shares: Whenever the management decides to cash out revenues (**condition**), dividends are distributed (**action**).

Heritage: The Smart Contract checks whether a person is alive (**condition**). If someone died, it handles the heritage (**action**).

Terminologies: Tokens, Coins, Currencies

A Blockchain allows to store data and Smart Contracts allow to perform actions or execute contracts on the Blockchain. Furthermore, units need to be used for calculations. And these units are sometimes currencies, sometimes tokens and sometimes coins. It is important to distinguish the three main types of units on Blockchains:

Cryptocurrency or Coin

Introductory: Getting started with the Blockchain

A cryptocurrency is used as a matter of exchange or payment (this is my personal definition, opinions vary). The focus lies on using the unit as value. When the term *coin* is used, the unit with an own Blockchain is meant, e.g. the Bitcoin is a coin and the *Bitcoin-Blockchain* is the Blockchain technology behind it.

- Example: Bitcoin. The coin is used to pay goods and store value. It does not have an "internal value" due to an asset it is backed by apart from trust into this currency.

Coins are characterized by the fact that they are not backed by any asset. Their price is usually formed out of supply and demand mechanisms, basically built upon the trust people are having into this currency.

Token
"Tokens are a representation of a particular asset or utility, that usually resides on top of another blockchain" [1].

In contrast to a cryptocurrency, a token was invented with a specific use-case in mind while a cryptocurrency is a general payment method for any kind of payment.

- Example 1: The Ethereum Blockchain was built in order to execute Smart Contracts on it. The network of miners behind Ethereum that are operating it needs to be incentivized, hence the ETH token was invented and is used to pay for the execution of Smart Contracts.

---

[1] https://masterthecrypto.com/differences-between-cryptocurrency-coins-and-tokens/

Introductory: Getting started with the Blockchain

If the user e.g. performs the transfer of an asset, he has to pay a fee in ETH. This token serves the purpose of keeping up a platform with its operations.

- Example 2: A token for a house in New York City. This token represents the asset. If the rent Is paid, it will be distributed between the token holders.

What is a token?
Tokens in the context of a Blockchain are referred to as **units that represent something**. Unlike a currency, they do not only serve as a matter of exchange and payment. They rather portray an object, may it be physical or virtual, on this digital unit. A token therefore could represent a house (as mentioned above). In this case the issuer would hand out e.g. 100 tokens where one token equals the right to one percent of the revenue generated by this property.

Since the term "token" is kept very general, it could literally represent everything. A short list of examples makes it more tangible:
- A token representing the share in a company
- A token representing physical gold
- A token representing the right to use a service
- A token representing the ownership of art or music

What this small excerpt of examples shows is that, technically speaking, **a token is nothing more than a unit stored on a distributed ledger** – which brings certain advantages that are discussed within the next pages. The most important question however is which rights this token is bound to. This is a more legal than a technical question.

Introductory: Getting started with the Blockchain

Just handing out a token is comparable to printing paper notes that are supposed to represent the ownership of an object. An artist may hand you a paper which should serve as a proof that you possess the original piece of art and you could physically obtain it by showing the paper. By just having this paper, it will be difficult for any third person to validate that the note or proof is real. If someone has stolen the piece of art and you report it to the police, you have to prove that you are actually the owner of it. Having the piece of paper from the artist may be enough of a proof, however the police would carefully need to check if the signature of the artist is original and you did not fake the document.

Furthermore, the artist could have also faked the note on his own behalf and handed out a faked drawing. Two issues are arising in this case:

- **The trust issues**
  The transaction requires the people to trust each other. The buyer has to believe that the note handed out by the artist is a real one and that the artist will accordingly hand out the art at a later stage.

- **The verification issues**
  Even if the note is correct, third parties may be skeptical when they see it. There is no secure way of checking the validity of the document – the third person can only believe that the signature on the paper is real.

These disadvantages being solved are some of the positive elements that the use of distributed ledgers bring and the reason why assets are tokenized. By using a token, trust is ensured, and a verifiable *proof of ownership* or *proof of a right is issued*. Any buyer who wants to buy the art without physically obtaining it could receive the token on the Blockchain: nobody can manipulate the transaction afterwards and a third-party such as the police or the court can verify its correctness to take legal action when it was stolen, or illegal activities have been conducted.

Summary: Blockchain, tokens, coins and cryptocurrencies

Distributed ledger technologies (DLT) are databases that are spread through many participants and operated by them. This allows users to interact with each other in situations when no trust exists, or the users do not know the counterparty. The users form a *consensus* and thereby ensure that they do not cheat on each other. The Blockchain is a special type of a distributed ledger in which the information is stored within blocks that are connected to each other.

DLT is the overall technology subject, Blockchain is one type of it that is again split into *public* and *private*. Those categories then split up again into different, specific Blockchains.

While cryptocurrencies were made to serve as a currency, tokens have more functionality and therefore are also referenced as *programmable money*. A token, as such, can serve for many purposes: It can be a native currency that is directly integrated into a product, a representation of an asset or used as a matter of exchange since they are easily transferable.

Tokenization

Simply revising, a token is a unit stored on a Blockchain. It can serve as a currency or as the representation of any object. The term tokenization means the process of creating this token on the Blockchain for an object that already exists.

How tokens become assets

A token, roughly speaking, basically becomes an asset by being used as a representation for such. People store information on the Blockchain that is supposed to be legally binding to represent the ownership of something (e.g. real estate) or the right for something (e.g. receiving dividends). Hence, a token is strictly bound to an asset and shall represent value.

From the technical point of view, a token is just a unit on the Blockchain. From the legal point of view, it represents something – for example gold. The legal and regulatory considerations are very important, so that they have been given an own chapter within the book.

Tokenization

Token   Represents   **Asset**

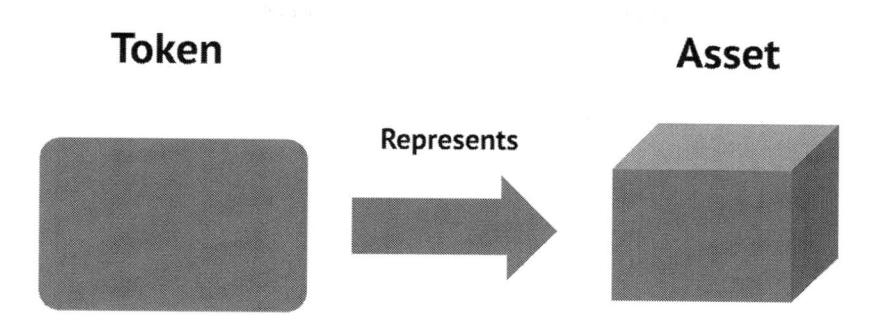

As illustrated, the token represents an asset. The arrow within the graphic indicates that the same token always points to the same asset.

That means if the token is transferred, the owner of the asset also changes. Whoever possesses the token shall possess the asset behind. This might sound obvious but is actually a legal challenge to implement. It needs to be ensured that the token counts as a valid and legally binding representation. If the token can be transferred, but the owner at a time cannot legally enforce his ownership rights within the jurisdiction (e.g. via court), the token is not useful.

Every action happening on the Blockchain (with the token) has to be legally enforceable in the real world.

It gets actually a bit more complicated than illustrated above. In reality, there has to be a bidirectional relation between the token and the underlying asset. So, if the asset is transferred, the respective token has to be transferred and vice versa. Hence, we should replace the arrow with a bidirectional connector between asset and token. Only then, it can be ensured that:

- When the token is transferred, the legal entitlement or ownership of the asset is transferred
- When the legal entitlement or ownership of the asset is transferred, the token is transferred

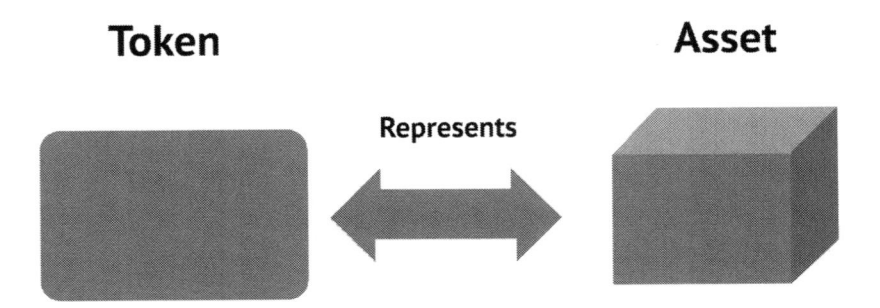

Token   **Represents**   **Asset**

Summarizing it, a token *becomes* an asset in our understanding when A) the underlying asset is represented by an implemented token and B) the legal enforceability of the token ownership equal to the asset ownership is given.

The advantages of tokens

A few of the advantages and arguments to use a token have been implicitly mentioned above. The argumentation in the following shall name both positive and negative aspects of tokens so that an objective decision whether tokenizing certain assets makes sense or not can be taken.

Tokenization

Trust
Ensuring that a note given out is still valid tomorrow is achieved by using a distributed ledger, since information that is stored on a Blockchain once is inerasable and immutable. Once the note (in this case the token) is transferred on the Blockchain, it can be traced.

Verification
Speaking of traceability, the token transfer is transparent. The owner of the asset can prove that he actually owns the asset or holds certain rights attached to it by showing the token being on his "account". Diving into the technical details at this point would shift the focus away from the topic of this book – simply speaking, the buyer of the art has a *wallet* that he can open with a password (the *private key*) and prove he possesses the respective token which then would prove the ownership of the art.

Fractional Ownership
Speaking of different assets, fractional ownership is made available the first time in history to this extent. Owning a real estate property with 10 persons requires a huge effort for legal contractions and notary work to ensure the rights the investors have, not even imagining the process for 100 or 1,000 investors. With security tokens, you could almost issue infinitesimal small units of assets and possibly allow 10,000 people to invest in a property together. The same goes for any other asset such as art, cars, collectibles or companies.

Access to global capital markets
...that is not bound to a specific jurisdiction or location. Unlike legal contracts, tokens are not implemented differently for every single jurisdiction. Once the token is implemented with an

interoperable token standard, it can easily be adopted worldwide and integrated into different distribution platforms. Compliance with the different jurisdictions needs to be ensured.

Lean Clearing & Settlement of transactions
The clearing and settlement, simply speaking the execution of transactions, is done on the Blockchain. There is no consortium of banks that needs to maintain a large infrastructure in order to do so.

Worldwide and time-zone-independent operations
The worldwide scalability of primary and secondary markets enables a globalized network, the operations can be kept on in different places within different time zones.

Lower barriers to invest into assets
Due to the efficiency advantages within the offering and settlement of securities, it is possible to accept and process much smaller payments from (retail) investors. Accepting smaller amounts of money might be possible with Crowdfunding platforms as well; however, those generally charge higher fees on the investments – typically three to seven percent[1].

Lower entry barriers for asset tokenization in the company's perspective
The fact that issuing a tokenized security requires less stakeholders, is technically faster and therefore cheaper, lowers the following barriers significantly:

---

[1] https://maxkops.de/comparing-crowdfunding-and-ico-fees-commissions/

- **Volume**
  Since the cost and time needed for an issuance is much lower, launching a tokenized security equivalent to e.g. a stock becomes an option to many more companies that would not consider going that path within the traditional finance system. An IPO is either too expensive or the relative effort is too high for them.

- **Cost**
  Efficiency gains make the field more competitive and enable lower costs of issuance due to the elimination of middlemen and no brokerage and investment banking fees[2].

- **Time and Operation**
  Since less stakeholders require less communication and the technical issuance process can be automated to a large extent, the time needed from the decision till the execution of an issuance is reduced.

Liberating the market
Banks and financial institutions that exist since **centuries** had a big monopoly or oligopoly when it comes to financial services and the issuance of financial products. With tokens, the technical process of the issuance is mainly driven by a Blockchain and can be done by agencies much easier. It still requires the corresponding licenses to do so, however new players in the market that offer a security token issuance are shaking up the monopoly and therefore create a price competition which is beneficial for

---

[2] https://cointelegraph.com/explained/what-is-an-sto-explained

the issuing company. It is also believed that using an asset backed token enables more precise valuation methods[3].

It is a general question (that could fill several books alone) whether the issuance of securities based on a token can be done without the assistance of the traditional financial industry. At the end, a bank is still needed to securely store the monetary funds.

It is much more likely that the existing structures within the financial industry will be shaken up and dramatically change, but they will not be fully replaced or become unnecessary any time soon. Rather, financial service providers ad institutions can encompass the new technology to expand their business model. The middle way with less stake holders, more efficient processes and eventually a smaller work force and a smaller power of the previous oligopoly industry are much more likely to be the future.

Secure storage
In the long run, a majority believes that the consensus algorithms can sustain a higher security for storing information within a network of stakeholders. Hence, storing assets on a Blockchain in the form of a token is much safer and less affective to a single point of failure that traditional, centralized systems sometimes have.

Easier post-offering administration
Security tokens can be much easier to be administrated after the actual issuance. Smart Contracts can automate many things that

---

[3] Maas, Thijs – Initital Coin Offerings: When Are tokens Securities in the EU and US?, 2019, p. 24

previously required repetitive administrative or notary efforts such as dividend payments.

Once the requirements and terms are defined, the lawyers' or notaries' decision can be translated into a smart contract and the execution of it can be technically ensured.

The disadvantages of tokens

No clear Regulation
Just representing an asset with the help of a token instead of other record keeping methods will not set anyone free of complying with the Regulation. A tokenized company share therefore should be required to fulfil the same requirements that a non-tokenized company share does. Nowadays, it could even be more difficult to issue a tokenized asset since many jurisdictions are not explicitly or implicitly considering tokens as a valid mean of keeping ownership records of the asset. However, in the future a more feasible process is expected due to the establishment of standards. Once this is done by regulators, the legal part becomes easier and faster when offering tokenized assets than with non-tokenized ones.

Lacking usability
Tokens might sound very innovative and promising to many investors, however most of them are not familiar with the technology behind. This makes it a bit more difficult to securely store the assets. Since the investor – in contrast to a bank – owns the assets himself, he is responsible for securing them securely and cannot automatically rely on a bank to manage them.

No sophisticated infrastructure

The infrastructure for security tokens is still being built. Experts often expect that by 2020 the first feasible infrastructure to issue and trade security tokens in an efficient way will be built. At the moment, the liquidity of decentralized exchanges is not sufficient[4] and most of the exchanges that want to offer security token trading are not yet operational because they are awaiting a regulatory approval. Once these approvals have been given out to several platforms, the ecosystem can evolve, and a few key players will turn out to be trustworthy.

Many security issues can be avoided by relying on proven offering platforms.

Bad aspects about removing the middlemen

Removing middlemen in the process of issuing securities seems to offer huge efficiency gains, however, it also removes experienced parties that had different roles. For example, classical financial institutions were not only responsible for their services they offered, but they also ensured a high level or security and regulatory compliance with sophisticated due diligence processes.

Handing the market over to the new players that might not be as experienced as the traditional institutions would mean going a step back in terms of experienced players.

Unclear governance, processes and structures

Especially the aspect of fractional ownership brings up new requirements that oftentimes cannot be adapted from well-known

---

[4] https://blockonomi.com/tokenizing-financial-assets/

systems. Enabling fractional ownership for assets like real-estate or art will need adjustments in the process, infrastructure and the Regulation. Governance is the key word expressing the need for set structures that define *who* is responsible for *what* when assets are tokenized.

Reputation of Blockchain
Although security tokens are not very comparable to cryptocurrencies or utility tokens, many people put all these terms into the same box. Which also means the bad reputation ICOs had or cryptocurrencies in certain regions still have due to the media is mixed up onto security tokens as well. Hence, some countries are taking an avoiding position towards security tokens or even banned them.

Summary

Tokenization means that assets are stored on a Blockchain and they are represented by a token. This enables fractional ownership due to the efficient processes and leads to a liberation of the market. This also brings up new regulatory challenges and requirements.

A few examples of tokenization

    real estate
    art and collectibles
    time
    physical goods and precious metals

Case Study: Tokenization of Real Estate

This case study practically shows a use case in which tokens are making a market more liquid, accessible and liberal. The focus completely lies on the **tokenization** itself, not on the actual Initial Offering like a STO.

> Lisa is a passionate mother of two lovely children aging six and eight years. She wants to enable her children pursuing their dreams and saved 10,000 US-Dollar for each child that they are supposed to be given once they finish high school. Lisa is not familiar with stocks but has a decent knowledge about properties since she is an architect. After doing some research, Lisa quickly realizes that with 10,000 US-Dollar she will neither be able to buy a property, nor is it enough money to finance a property with a loan from the bank. Simply speaking, she is excluded from the whole asset class of direct real estate. The cheapest property she found in her area had a price tag of 160,000 US-Dollar.

Case Study: Tokenization of Real Estate

Real Estate is an asset class that is well-known and easy to understand for everybody. It is an investment that everybody knows about and the specifics are quite easy to understand: A property such as a house is bought and the owner profits of monthly rental payments. Apart from speculation that this real estate object might increase in value due to external factors.

The issue whatsoever is that the access to real-estate investments is quite limited. Buying a property usually requires a large sum of money that needs to be paid upfront. Other options are loans from the bank and mortgages. In any case, you at least need savings that, calculating with an average salary, would take a couple of months or years for an individual to save. Most probably, the individual would not invest that money into other assets classes while saving for the property payment. Hence, the capital is bound without generating returns – which is, especially during low interest rate times, also a pity for the individual.

What if this market could be made more liquid in order to leverage more capital and earlier invest into real estate as an individual?

> Lisa comes up with the idea that she can buy the property together with a few friends. Sharing the property with sixteen persons is possible when everybody invests 10,000 US-Dollar. Now Lisa can afford investing into the chosen property.

Case Study: Tokenization of Real Estate

> She must be able to liquidate her share of the property in order to obtain the cash and give it to her child at a specific point. She also realizes that she would need to sell it to another person and have a meeting with the notary that signs this transaction. This will cost her a lot of money and time and it will be difficult to find an investor for this specific property with the specific share of it.

Breaking this question down, the following requirements would need to be met in order to enable such investments for people like Lisa.

A) The required minimum amount of invested money needs to be small (low monetary barrier)
B) The costs associated with an investment need to be low so that smaller investments are worth to accept (cheap process)
C) The effort to keep track of the owners or shareholders of the property shall be associated only with small costs
D) The asset shall be flexible and liquid

> Lisa heard of so-called tokens, small calculatory units on a Blockchain that represent her share of the property. Everybody who holds one unit of this token is entitled to receive one portion of the revenues earned with that property. There are exchanges where she can sell those tokens at any time. In order to liquidate her share as soon as her daughter graduates, Lisa decides to buy a token that is or will be listed on a public exchange. People can buy a small fraction there as well and do not have to spend time and money on notary work.

Case Study: Tokenization of Real Estate

Can a token make real estate investments more accessible?

Instead of rephrasing the general advantages of tokens as an asset representation, we can now outline the defined requirements with the knowledge obtained.

> *A) The required amount of money to be able to invest needs to be small (low monetary barrier)*

By fulfilling step *B: having small costs*, it is possible to accept smaller investments as well without having a big delusion due to the fees.

> *B) The costs associated with an investment need to be low so that smaller investments are worth to accept (cheap issuance process)*

Implementing a token is a very lightweight process and the token itself is not very complex in terms of the functionality. Once a token is developed, this implementation can be replicated for many different properties.

The more it is standardized and automated, the more notary costs can be eliminated that would otherwise occur. This makes the process fast, lightweight and cheap.

> *C) The effort to keep track of the owners or shareholders of the property shall be associated only with small costs (cheap maintenance)*

Instead of managing the list of owners or shareholders manually, a token would replace this ownership management.

Case Study: Tokenization of Real Estate

Not only can the token be used to manage the ownership, it can also be programmed so that revenues (in this case rental payments) are distributed between the owners. The extent of automation can lead so far that the rental payment only needs to be sent to a Smart Contract. This Smart Contract is not just defining the contract specifics but can also execute them. Hence, if the rental payment is collected, the smart contract can distribute it between the shareholders without a need of manual intervention.

D) The asset shall be flexible and liquid

Tokens can be divided into fractional units by nature and the issuer can limit how fractionable an asset it. Having an asset that can be divided into small pieces, both investors and issuers are profiting of a more liberal market:

An investor might buy one percent of a property, enabling him to invest in real estate with an amount as low as 500 US-Dollar.

After the property has been financed and sold to many different investors, they can easier manage their portfolio. While they previously would have needed to sell the complete property or a large portion of it in order to liquidate their assets, they can now sell very small fractions. What has been possible for stocks and financial products or real estate funds is now possible for a single property.

If you hold a portfolio of different real estate properties or an asset manager manages many different assets including real estate, rebalancing the portfolio is a matter of seconds.

Case Study: Tokenization of Real Estate

After doing further research, Lisa stumbles upon a specific offer in her area. It is the first offering of the company and hence limited to 16 investors. The investment is split up into 16 tokens, hence each token costs 10.000 US-Dollar. Together, all 16 people that do not even need to know each other can fully finance the property with the 160,000 US-Dollar of costs.

Lisa decides to buy a share. Finally, she is able to invest 10,000 US-Dollar solely into one, self-selected property in her area.

Is the tokenization of real estate already possible?
Some people might argue that investing into real estate with smaller amounts of money or sharing a property with different investors is already possible. Indeed, both of it is possible, however to a very different extent.

Sharing a property could for example be done by having **a company as a vehicle** in between that hold the properties. For example, you would have an own company that fully owns a specific building. Now, the investors own shares of the company. Any revenues made with the property would apparently flow into the company which then distributes it between the shareholders. Hence, ownership of a property with other investors is possible, however a very complicated process. Usually, a notary has to be included whenever a transaction is made. This also makes it almost impossible to have many different stakeholders involved

Case Study: Tokenization of Real Estate

at a reasonable cost level. These companies are called Special Purpose Vehicles (SPV).

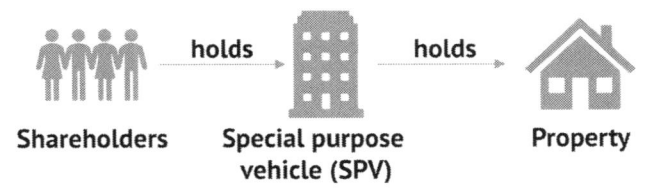

Shareholders —holds→ Special purpose vehicle (SPV) —holds→ Property

Crowdfunding for properties does exist, but buying very small fractions is usually not possible and a secondary market liquidity is not given so that people could easily sell their shares

Indeed, buying portions of real estate or crowdfunding properties is possible, but at a very basic level.

What are the challenges of tokenizing real estate?
In order to represent the ownership of real estate with a token, a specific *Regulation* would significantly enhance the process. When a SPV is needed that can then be tokenized, the operational costs of the company make the process a bit more costly. As soon as real estate can directly be tokenized, efficiency gains can be realized drastically.

> Lisa just leaves her own house in the morning and gets to know about a pipe break in the neighbor's house – the property she invested in and bought the token of. In the investors group, she sees that people are already discussing the issue – nevertheless, none of the 500 investors of the property actually feels responsible to fix it or get it fixed by a specialist. Lisa decides to call the specialist and pay him out of her pocket.

Case Study: Tokenization of Real Estate

Apart from Regulation, the internal *Governance* is a challenge to be solved. There must be a responsible party that is responsible for daily operations and the maintenance of properties. Practically speaking, someone has to roll up his sleeves to fix the water pipe quickly when problems occur. In a company, the CEO has the responsibility. It has to be defined how the responsible persons for property maintenance can be selected and if voting rights shall be attached to the tokens.

> Paying the bill for the water pipe fixing specialist was frustrating for Lisa since she cannot easily get the money back in portions from 16 different investors. Doing some research, she now gets to know about another company that offers a new, different token type for real estate with voting rights: A clear role structure is defined in terms of who has which responsibilities and just leaves her own house without having further responsibilities.

Summary: Tokenizing real estate
Tokenizing real estate is technically possible in an easy way for a single property. What is expected to be built within the next months and years is the infrastructure to tokenize real estate objects with a few clicks that allows to attach it to the legal documents – as well as Regulations keeping up and establishing a solid framework for tokenized real estate.

Then, the real estate asset class becomes significantly more accessible and liberal.

Initial Coin Offerings and Security Token Offerings

Everything described so far was related to general considerations about tokenizing assets. When it comes to the issuance process itself, e.g. of company shares, we are speaking about Security Token *Offerings* (STOs).

Back in times, Initial Coin Offerings (ICOs) were invented to finance Blockchain startups that sold their voucher like tokens for a service in the future. The focus of this book strictly lies on STOs, however ICOs will be depicted in order to understand the evolvement of token offerings and general terms.

Initial Coin Offerings (ICOs): Raising money by selling tokens

Initial Coin Offerings (ICOs) were the projects once considered as the *new*, *rebellious* startups raising capital in a new and *exciting* way without relying on the back of any of the traditional stakeholders involved in Fundraising processes. This hype mainly existed in 2017 and 2018. Why is it that ICOs were able to bypass the regulators and almost all intermediaries to offer their token to investors or users?

Initial Coin Offerings and Security Token Offerings

From the technological perspective, ICOs consist of a token which serves as a *native matter of exchange*, *payment* and as an *access to the protocol*. Those products and tokens are usually built on top of an existing Blockchain.

Example
Ethereum is a Blockchain **platform**, allowing people to basically run any *smart contract* on their platform and build Blockchain applications. These applications then exist on the Ethereum platform and use the Ethereum protocol in the background.

A job application for example is providing the logic that is necessary to connect the worker with the person offering the job. This job platform then runs on top of the Ethereum platform. Ethereum, in this case, can be compared to an operating system: If you are using an application on your smartphone, the execution of it is built on the operating system such as Android or iOS. Oftentimes, you as the user, might not think about the operating system behind when you are using the application. The same applies for ICOs. The different applications launch an own token on an existing Blockchain (comparable to the operating system).

The token economy – How tokens replace fees
Taking a job application on Ethereum as an example, that raises the question about the incentive for an inventor who launches such a job application. Usually, fees paid to a Blockchain based platform are kept as low as possible or even at zero – the applications often exist especially because they remove an intermediary from the existing business model. Replacing the intermediary with a decentralized Blockchain platform might make the product competitive. Instead of a platform with a bunch of employees

Initial Coin Offerings and Security Token Offerings

behind, a platform built out of an ICO would handle those operations through an automatic protocol. And since there is not necessarily an intermediary between the user and the protocol, there are no fees that somebody needs to receive.

The fee structure might sound a bit confusing now, so we are looking at it with some graphics to explain the service and monetary flow.

How companies provide a service – without ICO

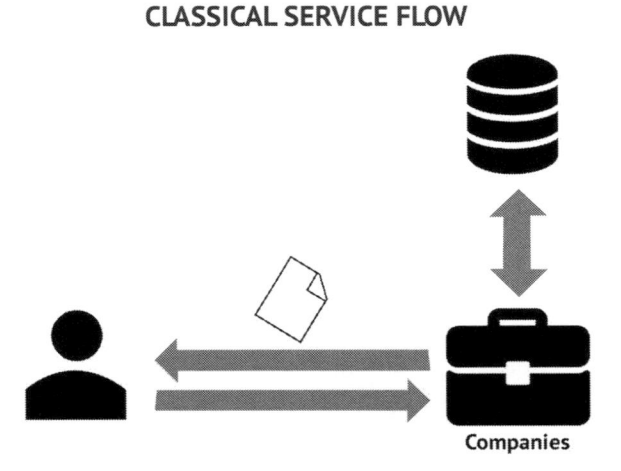

CLASSICAL SERVICE FLOW

Companies

As you can see in the graphic above, the company is *actively* providing the service and acts as an intermediary between the customer (left) and the actual service or value (top) – the reason why fees are necessary.

On the other hand, this is how the decentralized model looks like:

Decentralized service flow based on a protocol – with ICO

DECENTEALIZED SERVICE FLOW

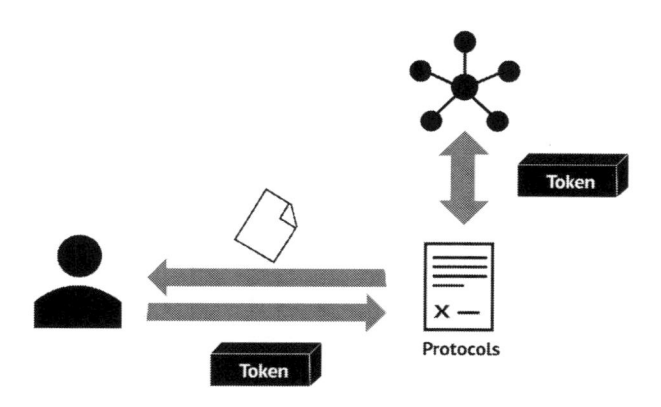

There is no company that is actively providing a service, instead a protocol is used. The intermediary, that creates costs due to the manual work, has been removed. Of course, the fees will never be literally zero because there has to be an infrastructure behind the service that needs to be compensated. You can see that the token is used to pay for the transaction costs occurring due to the execution of the protocol. The protocol forwards these fees to the decentralized network of people and machines that is providing the infrastructure and computational power. It is *not* given to the inventor or creator of e.g. the job application protocol. So, how does the inventor get incentivized?

Considering the profit point of view, we can summarize both scenarios as following:

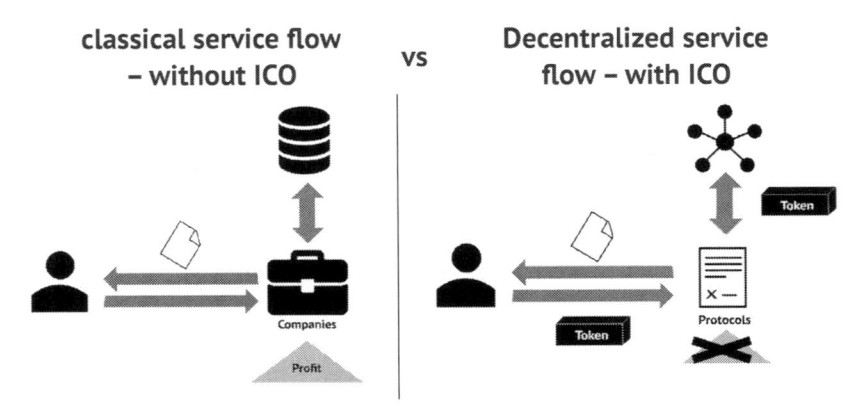

classical service flow – without ICO vs **Decentralized service flow – with ICO**

Decentralized service: The protocol is a digital entity and an *automated* set of rules and actions; therefore it does not have to generate revenues in order to cover the operational costs.

Classical service: Contrarily, a company is *actively* doing something to provide the service, may it be investing resources of any kind such as labor or work material, and therefore *needs* constant revenues to make profit.

How ICOs and their teams earn money

The business model of an ICO is the following: The tokens – sold for a *cheap* price – bring in the money that is needed to build the company with its products and services. Therefore, the tokens are sold upfront and before the service has actually been launched. A part of that money is used as a compensation for the team. While the founding team also holds a portion of the tokens, a preferably larger part is invested into the marketing and product development. Taking a cinema as an example, the initiator would sell cinema tickets for just one dollar although the cinema has not been launched. By selling five million tickets, he can cover the construction costs and pay himself a one-time compensation.

The ICO wild west: How ICOs escaped the Regulation

The reason I and many of my fellows are calling the ICO space that we have seen before early 2018 a *wild west* is the lack of Regulation. Most of the projects claimed to not fall under financial or securities Regulations since they thought they were just offering a voucher, an access to a network or a good – but not a security. By doing that, a single project could save hundreds of thousands of dollars, that would normally be spent for the complex construct required to issue securities.

How it started

There is a misbelief that Ethereum did the first ICO back in the days. Actually, the first ICO has already been performed in 2013 for the Mastercoin project. It was the first project that allowed investors to buy tokens as a native currency to use the protocol later on[1] [2].

In 2018, around 17 billion US-Dollar have been raised through ICOs. Undoubtedly, ICOs already passed their best time – this hype occurred between the end of 2017 and the beginning of 2018.

---

[1] Zynis, D. 2013 A Brief History Of Mastercoin
[2] https://blog.omni.foundation/2013/11/29/a-brief-historyof-mastercoin/. Accessed 19.08 19:44 a ICO_Market_Analysis_2018.pdf

Initial Coin Offerings and Security Token Offerings

At that time, many projects reached their funding goals but the quality of projects massively dropped and many investors made a profit by just buying into an ICO during the pre-sale and selling the obtained tokens a few weeks later on the secondary market[3].

While almost 10.1 billion US-Dollar have been raised through 718 ICOs in 2017, a significantly higher amount of 2518 ICOs raised no more than 11.6 billion US-Dollar in 2018. The amount of ended ICOs was 2.5 times higher than the year before while the funding only gained 15 percent. You can see below that all the three biggest ICOs ended in 2018[4].

Overview: The three biggest ICOs[5]

Project	Purpose	Money raised (USD equivalent)	Date
EOS	Infrastructure for decentralized applications	$4.2 billion	4th of June 2018
Telegram	A way to exchange money in a private messaging app	$1.7 billion	15th of February 2018
Petro	"Sovereign cryptoasset" Also referred to as a coin for Venezuela	$735 million	20th of April 2018

---

[3]   https://maxkops.de/ico-market-2018/
[4]   https://www.coindesk.com/ico-tracker 02.04 14:38
[5]   https://www.bloomberg.com/news/articles/2018-12-14/crypto-s-15-biggest-icos-by-the-numbers

Initial Coin Offerings and Security Token Offerings

Due to the fact that many people assumed laws and Regulations do not exist within the crypto space (which seemed to be reasonable since regulators did not yet have an eye on them at that time), ICOs were considered as the *wild west* of Fundraising. ICOs offered a super lightweight process of collecting capital from a large group of investors, comparable to Crowdfunding. Without even having to deal with the post-issuance tasks such as dividend payments. The tokens had their internal value since the market defined what a token was worth using it within the application or platform. If posting a job on the job application is worth five dollars for you, you would buy the token for every price up to five dollars.

At the same time, the investing parties enjoyed a very anonymous way of investing their money into startups. Only a few of them were implementing requirements to verify the identity of investors. Since most did not, the doors were open for money launderers and criminals to wash their money. As soon as ICOs gained more attention within the mainstream and somehow became popular, the regulators kept an eye on them and started fining projects that were violating laws such as the securities Regulations, financial services, etc.

However, it was unclear whether the tokens should be classified as securities or as simply goods or other objects. By claiming that a token is a voucher, a good, a ticket or similar, the projects tried to avoid falling under securities laws. Especially in the beginning of 2018 more and more projects feared regulatory interventions and consequences when performing an unregulated tokensale. For example, in January 2018 the U.S. Securities and Exchange

Commission (SEC) was intervening in the biggest supposed ICO at that time. Another shutdown of two ICOs by the SEC has been announced by the end of 2018 since they "each broke U.S. securities laws"[6]. The Munich startup Rise.eco promised "passive income" and got shut down in the end of 2018[7]. Similar cases could be found all over the world and the projects began to become skeptical about the traditional ICO as a matter of Fundraising. Hence, many projects wanted to align their ICO at the classical securities laws and launch something that is more similar to a security than to a product, voucher or ticket. At this time, the term "security token" was born for regulated tokens that were classified as securities by law.

Good aspects of the ICO wild west
During the time ICOs were under the radar of governments and regulators it could be proved that the community has a demand for crowdinvesting possibilities especially into Blockchain startups. The idea of an ICO was simply born by selling a utility upfront when the respective service did not even exist yet – therefore the user buys access to the platform upfront (hopefully) for a cheap price. Some projects still seemed to be serious about their vision a year later while other projects gave up their plans. Without the hype around ICOs, the topic of security tokens probably would not be as famous as it is now.

---

[6] https://www.theblockcrypto.com/2018/11/17/the-sec-cracks-down-on-two-icos-creates-a-template-for-future-enforcement/
[7] https://www.gruenderszene.de/fintech/rise-bafin-ico?interstitial_click

Bad aspects of the ICO wild west

A wild west is known for freedom as well as for crime. Hence, a load of bad stories and ICO scandals can be found.

Since the space of ICO initiators was not following Regulations, scamming people was a comparingly easy game for criminals. Since the user could just sent his money to a service and they in return sent him tokens, this also allowed for many manipulations and attacks. Cases occurred in which thousands of investors were sending their money to a project that was not existing – even the team profile pictures were stolen. Fear of missing out (FOMO), being unexperienced in financial investments and solely relying on the intelligence of the crowd were probably some of many reasons that led to scams like this as a combination of them.

> **Outlook: Initial Exchange Offerings**
>
> Another possibility of issuing the token is through an exchange. In this case, the exchange not only provides the trading facility, but also enables people to initially buy the tokens. These so-called Initial Exchange Offerings (IEOs) are very new and hence just emerging. At the time of writing, there are no IEO options for security tokens yet – however I believe they are going to be created within the next months when a few exchanges established their compliant operation. Combining the primary and the secondary market contradicts the idea of decetralization, but can release efficiency gains.

Link Code: 1

Case Study: The difference between ICOs and STOs

The example I use to explain ICOs and STOs in my speeches and workshops is building a cinema. Given the plan of building a cinema and the assumption that the company wants to utilize a Blockchain-driven way of fundraising, they have two options: Issuing a utility token (ICO) or issuing a security token (STO).

Building a cinema with an ICO

An ICO from an investors point of view
The investor is convinced that the cinema will be successful and can attract a lot of customers. He estimates that a customer would be willing to pay five dollars to watch a movie. Therefore, he buys *utility* tokens, which in this case would mean cinema tickets.

Since the cinema is not built yet, it hands out those tickets that can be redeemed in the future for just two dollars. If the investors assumption of customers paying five dollars for a ticket is correct, he could make a profit of three dollars by selling his ticket once the cinema is built.

An ICO from an startups point of view
Instead of handing out equity (share of the company) or specific shareholder rights, the company (in this case the cinema) is giving out *objects attached to a right for future usage*. This could be the access to a network, the access to certain content or a voucher-like promise. In the case of the cinema, the utility tokens seem to be most comparable to a voucher/ticket that can be used to enter the cinema at a later stage.

Initial Coin Offerings and Security Token Offerings

The founders actually get paid upfront before they have set a single stone in the ground for the cinema. Most of the money raised will be invested into building the cinema and a small part used to incentivize the initiators. However, if they want to gain more profit by increasing the token price (since they also own a portion of the tokens) they are motivated to drive the project into a successful direction. Unfortunately, this motivational structure has led to projects using unethical methods to increase the token price.

How is an ICO different from classical fundraising?

The business model behind an ICO is usually quite different from the motivation founders have when they establish a new startup or company. Instead of hoping to gain profits due to possessed equity and the related portion of the revenues, an ICO team has two income streams as mentioned above:

1) A portion of the raised funds

2) A portion of the tokens

As you can see, no revenues that are made upon the launch and operation of the service are included. This is quite contradictive to the case of classical equity fundraising in which the founders would get a share of the ongoing revenues. In the case of an ICO, one part (1) is paid one-time and upfront, while part (2) is paid in tokens and indirectly influenced by the value the service is providing. It is assumed that the better the service or product is, the more people are willing to pay for the token. Hence, providing an excellent service is in the interest of the founders to possibly increase the value of the token.

Initial Coin Offerings and Security Token Offerings

On one hand the feasible way of trading tokens and liquidating them is an important advantage of token-related business models. On the other hand, it led to *wrong* motivations within the founding team to simply increase the token price with unethical methods such as market manipulation.

What are Security Token Offerings?

The example of the cinema above explained how ICOs work. As you have read there, the *utility tokens* were used to represent a voucher or generally a right for future usage of a service. Therefore, it seems to be quite different from traditional financial products that startups or enterprises could issue. Doing exactly that leads us to the opposite side of ICOs and *utility tokens*: **Security tokens** are referred to as tokens that actually do promise certain rights and should be similar to e.g. a share in a company. Therefore, the kind of fundraising is the same, but the technology behind is different and now done with a token instead of classical agreements. Simply speaking, the shares that previously existed on a paper signed by a notary now exist on a Blockchain in the form of tokens. This does not only count for company shares, but also for real estate, oil, precious metals, art and may other assets.

As soon as we speak about security tokens, we are calling the issuance process a **Security Token Offering (STO)** – only when utility tokens are issued, the term Initial Coin Offering (ICO) is used. Getting back to the example of the cinema makes this comparison easily understandable:

Initial Coin Offerings and Security Token Offerings

Aspect / Type of token	Security Token – STO	Utility Token – ICO
Investors perspective	Investors buy a share of the cinema	Investors buy a coupon for free entry to the cinema *** CINEMA Free Entry
Motivation for investment	High revenues *lead to* High cashout for shareholders	Higher demand *leads to* Higher ticket (token) price *leads to* Investor making a *one-time* profit by selling the token
Customer perspective	Customer enters the cinema and pays the price for a ticket.	Customer buys the ticket before entering on a marketplace from the investor.

The customers perspective can have a huge impact on the usability of a Blockchain based service and is one of the major topics I am discussing with my consultancy clients. The visitor of the cinema does not want to buy a voucher before and use a third-party for that, but simply enter the cinema and pay for the service. Whenever such a token is issued, it must be very easy to buy and be accessible by future users. However, the usability considerations would lead to far from the actual topic of this chapter.

Overview of different terms

ETO
The abbreviation ETO means *Equity Token Offering*. Such tokens shall represent real equity of a startup, meaning that the ownership of such a token would be equal to having equity of the company.

TGE
The abbreviation TGE means *Token Generation Event*. Hence, it describes the offering of any kind of tokens. Since it is not an initial offering, it could also embrace the tokenization of existing assets.

ICO
The abbreviation ICO means *Initial Coin Offering* and refers to the sale of utility tokens.

STO
The abbreviation STO means *Security Token Offering* and refers to the sale of tokenized securities, hence tokens that are representing a regulated security of any kind, such as equity.

IEO
The abbreviation IEO means *Initial Exchange Offering* and refers to the initial sale of tokens through an exchange. The primary market is then handled by an exchange which is then also the secondary market to trade the tokens at a later stage[8].

Many more abbreviations can be found that are not widely used and represent one of the forms above.

---

[8] https://www.binance.vision/glossary/initial-exchange-offering

When to STO and when not to STO

It is falsely believed that STOs will replace *any* other kind of Fundraising. It is likely that many assets or even almost all of them will be tokenized in the future. However, that does not necessarily require a Security Token **Offering** as we know it nowadays. In many cases, a project might be better off by privately raising capital (first) and considering an STO for a later stage.

Coming back to the present, which we refer to as the years 2019 and 2020, an STO might not be the Fundraising approach of choice for some projects. As depicted in the Regulatory chapter, the treatment of STOs by regulators remains unclear in many jurisdictions. This is one negative aspect to consider when deciding for or against the launch of a security token. On the other hand, the dynamic ecosystem can provide a healthy and fast-growing ground for other startups.

The technical, legal and economic infrastructure for the security token ecosystem is in early stages. This requires more effort from projects since a lot of it needs to be done individually – the topic is new for many involved stakeholders. Especially lawyers are facing uncertainty and hence have to invest a lot of time into the project in order to pave the way for a compliant offering. Taking into consideration that legal fees are in some regions paid upfront, without or with just a little success fee, this means more costs are ramping up.

Is it too early for an STO?
At the time of writing (May 2019), more and more projects are preparing their offering of tokenized securities. The secondary market environment is quite empty – most of the exchanges are waiting for their regulatory approval. Therefore, the question whether it is too early to launch an STO, seems reasonable to be asked.

It is obvious that conducting a STO in a few years will be easier and faster, but this should not be the only reason to postpone or neglect the option of conducting a STO in 2019 or 2020. It is important to be aware of the dynamic environment and be prepared that things can change quickly. Taking this into account, even some first mover advantages may be realized. As you have and will probably read throughout this book, fundraising is about much more than just collecting money. It involves strategic aspects, marketing benefits and other leverages.

Summary: STO or NTO?
Summing it up: Does is make sense at the current time being to conduct an STO or is *No Token Offering* (NTO) the better approach?

Most important to consider for that decision is probably the financial structure (as discussed in *The process of STOs*). Depending on how much money shall be raised, in which period of time, from which types on investors and whether issuing a token has further, non-monetary benefits, an STO may be a viable option.

Another thing to keep in mind is the time it takes to perform an STO. Starting from the decision to perform an STO, it takes a couple of months until the necessary approvals are obtained, and the real offer can be performed. Since exchanges are currently working and competing on obtaining the licenses for trading security tokens, this challenge might be solved in a couple of months as well.

If the amount of capital to be raised is very low, facing the costs associated with a public offering of securities (tokenized or not tokenized) may not be reasonable. On the other hand, if capital is being raised from many different parties instead of a few (three to five) larger investors, a security token can significantly reduce the efforts for maintaining the shareholder structure in the traditional way with the help of a notary. Also, the ability of buying very fractional parts and being able to sell fractions of it on secondary markets later can be very important for investors to adjust their risk profile and have assets that are easy to liquidate.

Reading this chapter, you probably expect an answer in the form of YES or NO. But this is nothing that can generally be said by anyone having an interest of objectively taking this decision.

The chapter *Advantages and Disadvantages of Tokens* and *The Process of Security Tokens* will help outlining the aspects to base the decision on. With those aspects discussed, an internal meeting and a board meeting or the opinion of external Advisors can form the decision.

When to STO and when not to STO

The ecosystem for security tokens is being developed and a wide, efficient network of service providers, exchanges, and regulatory clearness will probably be available within the next 18-24 months.

Summary

Whether a STO is the best viable option for a company to raise money shall be decided carefully. Since there is a conflict of interest, issuance platforms sometimes recommend conducting a STO when it actually comes with high costs.
Therefore, investing a huge effort into evaluating the option of a STO can be very valuable afterwards.

You can learn more about your personal, free Consulting session at the end of the book.

Security Token Offerings in detail

Till this point of the book, the focus has been lying on the background, the history and the related topics of Security Token Offerings. This chapter elaborates specific and separate topics at a deeper level. Furthermore, these single aspects will be put together within the next chapter to create a procedural view on the process of a Security Token Offering.

The stakeholders in a STO

Issuer
The party that sells the securities and raises the money[1].

Issuance Platform
The issuance platform is the portal on which investors can register, verify their identity and ultimately invest in the project. While some projects individually develop this infrastructure, many rely on existing software to concentrate on their core business.

Team and Advisors

---

[1] https://www.investopedia.com/terms/i/issuer.asp

Security Token Offerings in detail

The STO needs an own team for the execution on top of the team that is working on the product. Hiring a few team members for the duration of the Offering preparation and a team of community managers (internally or externally) for customer support is a necessity. The same applies for STO Advisors that are structuring and strategically aligning the process of the STO and include their knowledge and experience to leverage the power of the team and accelerate the go-to-market strategy.

Early investors and syndicates
Similar to an IPO, a STO brings up many fixed costs that need to be covered before the actual Offering can be performed. In order to obtain these resources, early investors and syndicates are included.

Attorneys
The attorneys are taking care of complying with the respective Regulations and help obtaining the necessary approvals by the authorities.

Compliance Provider
Further providers that are performing verifications of registered investors and monitor the process as well as the investments in order to prevent fraudulent activities and money laundering.

Banks
It is important to have a bank access in place early on where payments and investments can be received. Similar to exchanges, banks (should) also conduct a very strict due diligence process. This detailed checkup of the company or venture raising money can take a long time, so obtaining a bank account shall be done in advance.

Classical banks have a more conservative attitude towards digital assets and may take a longer time to approve a project and create an account. On the other hand, offshore banks are subject to changes and might lack a solid reputation. Nonetheless, in concrete the projects, I have discovered that certain classical banks are taking a positive stance on tokenized assets.

Splitting the received funds between different banks can reduce the risk.

Security Token Exchanges / Secondary Markets

Exchanges, or the secondary market, is as important as the primary market (initial offering). When the tokens cannot be traded or sold by investors, there is no incentive in initially buying a token from the issuer.

The more liquidity exists, the easier it is to trade the tokens and execute trades in a reasonable timeframe. Ensuring that the issued token becomes a liquid asset is one of the main responsibilities of the token issuer. Getting the token listed on different exchanges enables a more active secondary market trading and potentially more transparent price developments.

At the time of writing, most of the exchanges are preparing or awaiting their approval by Regulators and authorities that they need to trade regulated securities. Since the exchanges are managing the money of their customers, the regulatory requirements are very high.

A list of selected exchanges that are operational or close to be launched is provided within the web portal.

Custody

Custody can be described as the service to hold "customers' securities for safekeeping in order to minimize the risk of their theft or loss"[2]. It is a service known from the financial world that can also be adapted for cryptographic assets such as tokens.

Speaking about tokens, the chapter *Getting started with the Blockchain* explained the concepts of the Blockchain and how users access their digital assets. Simply recovering that, a public key cryptography is used. This cryptography consists of two important keys to be possessed: The public key that can be revealed to anyone and serves as the address to receive tokens or cryptocurrencies. On the other side, the private key shall never be revealed since he is used to sign transactions made from that address, comparable to a password. Since there is no intermediary and solely the private key gives a person access to the funds, there is a risk of the key being lost or stolen. In order to minimize that risk (according to the aim of Custody), people instead use a centralized party that is storing these keys and consequently holds the crypto assets on behalf of them.

KYC and AML

Know-Your-Customer (KYC)

Projects need to make sure that they act on a legal basis and this includes the fact that they should for example only accept

---

[2]   https://www.investopedia.com/terms/c/custodian.asp

investments from trustworthy individuals and companies and neglect any payment involved in fraudulent activities[3].

This sets the pre-requirement to know who is investing in the project. In the business world, Know-Your-Customer, shortly KYC, has been established as the term for this process. The Customer (in this case the investor) has to submit all the credentials such as the address and passport information. After that, the validity has to be checked – usually done with a video call in which the investor would need to look into the camera while showing the passport.

All this is related to individuals. When a company is investing, this process is called *Know-Your-Business (KYB)*. The information submitted varies and e.g. includes the company information as well as the shareholders / beneficial owners if the investor is a company. Within the book, the term KYC will be used but embraces any activity performed to identify, verify and validate an investor.

Anti Money Laundering (AML)
The purpose of implementing KYC procedures is to know who is investing so that fraudulent activities are hoped to be prevented or the person conducting them can be traced. Governments specifically have in interest in preventing money laundering activities, hence Anti Money Laundering (AML) countermeasures are coming into place. With those, it shall not be possible for anyone to launder money through an investment in the project.

---

[3]   https://wirtschaftslexikon.gabler.de/definition/know-your-customer-prinzip-kyc-53389

Money laundering in this case, simply put, would consist of a person or an entity investing money that stems from criminal activities or corruption into the project. The tokens bought would then get sold again and the criminal could claim that the money has been faithfully earned by investing in this venture and is not coming from a previous criminal activity. This is exactly what should be impossible with correct AML implementations: For example, if larger amounts of money are invested, the source of funds would be obtained and checked for validity.

How do projects implement KYC and AML?
KYC and AML measures are a typical outsourcing case to third-party services that have a team of plenty of administrators available 24/7 to perform KYC checks. Maintaining a 24/7 operation to meet the different timezones of investors can be quite cost-heavy, so outsourcing that can save a lot of effort and money.

The same goes for AML: Some providers specified on AML solutions for companies involved in cryptocurrencies and DLT. If the investor invests in the form of cryptocurrencies, they can check their database and potentially detect cases in which funds that have previously been involved in criminal activities are moved.

STO vs. IPO

Since the term Security Token Offering and Initial Coin Offering is already an allusion to *Initial Public Offerings* (IPO), we will compare a STO with a classic IPO.

An IPO is the process of initially issuing shares of a company. Although it seems quite similar to an ICO or a STO, the process strictly varies. IPOs happen on a regulated basis within the traditional financial system, including banks. They do not involve a Blockchain or tokens. When a company is *going public*, it initially sells a portion of their shares on the stock market. The banking consortium, stock markets, Advisors and IPO underwriters are taking care of the offering.

STOs can be seen in two ways: Either as an alternative to an IPO, or as the IPO 2.0 – an evolution of the existing process. Is the STO really a digitized way of doing IPOs and can disrupt the industry with the many stakeholders involved in the process?

The goals of IPOs and STOs

The goal of a STO is to issue securities, for example shares of the company. Looking at the IPO definition above, they are very similar. Breaking it down, the goal stays the same while the way of achieving it differs.

Issuance	IPO	STO
Type of Security	Company Share	Company Share (etc.)
Record keeping method	Bank Register	Token on a Blockchain

Security Token Offerings in detail

What are the main differences between an IPO and a STO?

As the table above shows, the issuer or the company to be financed often wants to issue a financial product that is similar to the financial products of the traditional financial system. The only difference is that the record keeping about who owns how many parts of them and which transactions are made: Within the traditional system, banks are responsible to perform that record keeping with their centralized databases. The token-based approach relies on a decentralized network like a Blockchain that is managing the records.

Besides the method of record keeping, the stakeholders involved vary a little bit. Most of the stakeholders that are involved in an IPO are also required within a STO. The difference is that due to the decentralization, the market of service providers, banks and other stakeholders gets liberated. The record keeping that is being done by the bank in the case of an IPO is now fully outsourced to a Blockchain – this Blockchain does not need to be operated by the bank or the issuer. Hence, the service that needs to be provided by an issuer or the bank changes. It is less about implementing the actual record keeping and more about providing the infrastructure that enables the interoperability between the stakeholders and building a legal ground. For example, it must be made sure that the token is technically implemented in a way that allows exchanges to list it for trading. Simply speaking, many stakeholders of a STO are the same as in an IPO, but the number of them and their involvement especially from the financial institutions is much less.

Facts & Figures

Costs

Although there is not much of scientific evidence about the costs of a STO, they are typically lower than in the case of an IPO. While an IPO typically costs between 6-12% of the amount of money raised[4], the token-based funding only creates 5-10% of expenses[5].

Nowadays, conducting a STO involves a lot of uncertainty and manual work which increases the costs for Advisors, platforms and individual implementations. It can be expected that due to the possible automation within STOs and the interoperable infrastructure that is being built at the moment, these costs can be significantly lowered within the next years, maybe even decreasing them to 3-5% of the raised amount.

In both cases, fixed costs and costs associated with the raised amount of money are involved, hence larger offerings tend to be more efficient judging by their proportional costs.

Time

An IPO can be conducted in only 3-4 months[6] in Europe and can take 6-9 months within the US[7].

---

[4] http://www.ipobox-online.de/erlose-und-kosten-bei-einem-ipo/5-2-kosten-eines-ipos.
[5] Initial Coin Offerings als alternative Finanzierungsmethode zu Initial Public Offerings, Max Kops
[6] IPO-Management: Strukturen und Erfolgsfaktoren, B. W. Wirtz and E. Salzer, p. 44
[7] https://www.streetdirectory.com/travel_guide/18694/corporate_matters/going_public_how_long_does_it_take.html

Security Token Offerings in detail

Within a STO, there is a bit more of volatility, since the technology and infrastructure is still emerging. STOs usually require a longer timeframe of preparation. The timeframe from the decision of performing a STO and actually starting the public offering can take 9-12 months at the moment, highly depending on the jurisdiction. It is just a matter of time until regulators will establish respective rules for tokenized business models or existing assets getting tokenized.

Existing infrastructure
When it comes to the efficiency and the infrastructure in the present, IPOs clearly outperform STOs. While security tokens are a relatively new phenomena, IPOs are widely known for decades and have established a solid infrastructure of banks, syndicates and exchanges.

Efficiency
Speaking about the future, tokenized offerings are expected to be much more efficient than classical offerings for several reasons discussed earlier in this book such as:
- Fractional Ownership
- Lower barriers in terms of volume, cost and time
- Easier access to global capital markets

When to STO and when to IPO
The question when an IPO or a STO is the better way has to be answered very case specific. However, many readers showed their interest in getting this question answered, so simplifying it, this is the answer:

Security Token Offerings in detail

An IPO is in most cases appropriate for mature companies with a solid income stream or massive growth. It typically raises larger amounts of capital in hundreds of millions or in billions of dollars.

A STO is more lightweight and allows smaller companies to go public or utilize other means of financing their venture. It might also be relevant when the business operates in many different locations worldwide and wants to target their investors in a strategic way.

This comparison is only focusing on STOs vs. IPOs. Whether a STO is a good choice in general will be covered in the chapter *When to STO*.

Personal opinion: *Furthermore, this is my stance at the time of writing in July 2019. I strongly believe that in the long term, all assets will be tokenized and IPOs will become STOs.*

When to STO and when not to STO

The Process of Security Token Offerings (STOs)

This chapter conveys a practical approach and overview of the process how security tokens are being launched. It is kept easy to read and very close to the best practices on the market, rather than focusing on abstract literature. In addition to the other chapters highliting single aspects of security tokens, this chapter offer as procedural view with a focus on the order of the activities. The process starts with the business model definition and ends with a fully executed Security Token Offering.

The process of 18 steps we are going through here is a suggestion based on my experience, the experience of many contributors to the book, developers, professors, lawyers and experts my fellows and me met all over the world.

We are covering the general procedure that may vary depending on the asset being tokenized, the type of investors, the geographical target market, the jurisdiction, the technology, the maturity of the business and several other factors. It provides a general guideline rather than a fixed approach – a mandala that your team needs to paint.

The Process of Security Token Offerings (STOs)

If you have a look into books about IPOs for companies going public, you will find a very standardized procedure of going public. Each step is usually done in the same order throughout different projects and there is a clear overview about the stakeholders to include in a specific role at a given time.

Our aim is to provide the first standardized approach of conducting a STO with this book.

Please, once again, keep in mind that this is a personal opinion and it does not replace Consulting a lawyer for legal regards, as well as it is not financial advice.

1. Defining the business model

If a whole company itself is being tokenized, the business model needs to be defined in detail. The business model shall be communicated clearly for every aspect or part of the company that is having an effect on the token. It might be that an existing company only tokenizes a new business unit or a subsidiary. In this case, the business model of the unit to be tokenized must be understandable for investors. It might still be useful to also communicate information about the overall business operation or the mother company since it can give prospects the information whether the main business is strong and how the founders personally lead their company. Simply speaking, the more transparency a project provides, the better and easier it can be evaluated by others.

New companies generally require more effort to prove themselves to the market. They sell something that is not

The Process of Security Token Offerings (STOs)

built yet – rather a vision than a product. Hence, many people believe that a startup has to put a specific effort into showcasing their team. At the end, the information provided has to meet the investors criteria, so the following topics shall be a part of the story:
- Team
- Idea and product
- Market
- Roadmap
- Usage of the funds

The priority of each criteria is subjective and varies from investor to investor. This is only the first story that is built around the project and that can be shown e.g. on the website, during pitches and within an Executive Summary.

With this story, prospects who are interested in this project or company would then look at the details that we are going to define in the following.

> **Did you know?**
> Within the space of IPOs on the stock market, bankers used to speak of the *equity story*. This is the story developed in order to bring a company to the market and sell it to investors.

Legal requirements may force you to publish more or other information.

> **Result at the end of this step**
> The business model is clearly defined, and it is clear what exactly is being tokenized. The project's story is built to attract prospects.

2. Defining the token use-case (ICO) or the token structure (STO)

The token specification has to be defined at an early stage. Although we want to focus on STOs, we will briefly mention the main differences between ICOs and STOs in this step.

Depending on the specification of the tokens, the following steps might look very different. If a utility token shall be used, the whole process looks different.

ICO

When launching a utility token through an ICO, this token actually serves as a technical element. It is directly attached to the value proposition or the service the startup is providing. Hence, it is crucial for investors to analyze the *token specification* in order to evaluate the project.

The main question is: What is the token for?

If the path is set for a utility token, a *real* utility needs to be given. It must be redeemable for value, most often the access to a platform. Just hoping to avoid Regulation should not be a reason to pursue the launch of a utility token. In that case, the token most likely does not have a real use-case. And since there is no asset that is legally bound to the token, having no utility most probably means not having any value. This is why most of the ICOs lost a large portion of their value compared to the initial selling price. They simply did not create enough value that backs the token.

In the best case, a utility token has both a value delivered *due to the use of a Blockchain technology* (technological value) as well

The Process of Security Token Offerings (STOs)

as a value delivered *independently of which technology is used* (business value) to implement this project.

If the purpose of the new platform is to build a real-world gig economy, where people can execute simple jobs on, this business model can create value in two ways:

A) The value created for people who can now find a job in their area and people in the need of help for simple jobs getting connected. This value is created independently of the technology used – it is a business value. Whether it is a Blockchain, a different DLT or even a centralized database only matters to a certain extent.

B) By using the Blockchain, fees within the gig economy that are typically much higher on existing online-platforms with a different target group, can be drastically reduced. This value is created due to the fact a Blockchain is used and the intermediary hence is being kicked out of the process – this is a technological value.

Since we are focusing on STOs throughout this book, we will not discuss the details of designing a successful utility token model. *The ICO matrix* provides you with further considerations of utility token business models and can be found in the web portal.

Link Code: 2

Again, I want to raise the awareness that ICOs and STOs are completely different, if not even incomparable. ICOs are used when the token serves as a technical element, STOs rather offer a new technical method of issuing financial products.

The Process of Security Token Offerings (STOs)

STO

The business model of the venture itself is pretty independent from the token design in the case of security tokens. As explained in H*ow tokens become assets*, the token is only representing a certain right or the ownership of an asset. Hence, the asset behind is the most important aspect the investor probably cares about.

Considerations about how the token needs to be integrated within the product or network can be completely neglected.

Rather, classical evaluation methods and procedures of financial transactions have to be gone through. It must be very clear what the token offers and how it is structured. The type of financial asset shall not only be clear for the investor. It is also required to be defined anyhow since depending on the classification, certain Regulatory requirements are coming into place. Speaking from the process point of view, the following questions shall be answered at the very beginning:

Why *is the money being raised?* **How** *do we create value with that money?* **What** *is being offered to investors in exchange for X?*

The questions do not specifically refer to tokenized securities at all. It could be asked in the same way if a startup would raise money without ever touching a token or a Blockchain. Whatsoever, this is a necessary step that actually clarifies whether a security token is the right way to raise money at all.

When you are reading this book, you might have bought it with the intention of launching a STO. Still, with this step of the process, we have not reached the point yet at which the decision about executing a STO is the best possible way to go or not. All the considerations till now were of a general nature, independent of whether we are launching a STO or we will collect funds and give out equity in a classical way.

By answering the first question above, a first estimation of the costs and the time needed can be made by the lawyer and an experienced STO Advisor. The more this question is elaborated, the better the estimation may be. For example, *what* is offered to the investors in exchange for their investments reveals whether only institutional and accredited investors should be accepted, or the fundraising includes retail investors as well. This question again opens up very different Regulatory consequences. Targeting retail investors is much more complicated since the Regulator implements higher investor protection standards that e.g. within the European Union certain professional/institutional investors are excluded from. Breaking that down further and further, a conscious decision shall be taken whether a STO is the right way to go or not. In the chapter *The advantages and disadvantages of tokens* and *When to STO and when to NTO* we discussed a few pros and cons of STOs that are helpful to take this decision.

Assuming that a STO makes sense, the specifics of the token and the offering can be outlined.

Token Economics and elements of the token structure

Having defined the financial and business aspects, these information and requirements need to be translated into a specific structure for the tokensale, the so-called *token economics*. They specify all hard and soft facts and figures around the token – more or less the fundamentals. Hence, they are a very important criteria investors look at.

Soft Cap
The Soft Cap defines the minimal amount of money to be raised. If the funding round has ended and the money raised is less than the soft cap, the company party returns the invested money to investors (according to the contracts). Since launching the tokensale and bringing the project to this step costs some amount of money, not the whole sum can be returned to investors.

Hard Cap
The hard cap is the maximum amount of money to be raised. During 2018, some projects raised money without specifying a hard cap. While collecting more money looks like a sound idea, the additional value is decreasing by every monetary unit. Furthermore, the token shall represent a value – so the more money that is collected, the more value needs to be created. Otherwise, a higher investment (and probably more money spent) leads to the same value that is being delivered. If more money than needed is collected, this capital cannot be utilized and hence limits the overall return on investment. Many people believe that a higher early-stage funding for startups does not necessarily lead to better outcomes. For that reason, the hard cap should be set at a reasonable level.

Token Distribution
The token distribution however means the allocation between different stakeholders. The decision about how many tokens exist is usually less relevant than how they are allocated. Transactions made on the Blockchain can be fractional, so it does not

matter how many tokens are given out - only the relative share is important.

The main categories of people that get a portion of the tokens are:
- Founders
- The team
- Investors
- The advisory board

The token Distribution, the hardcap and the bonus structure are the most complex decisions a STO Advisor has to work on. Speaking about asset-backed tokens like real estate tokens, the token distribution and the bonus structure can set a project an investor would not invest in apart from one the investor would buy into.

In the context of stocks, people call this effect (stock) *dilution*[1]:

If the token is backed with real estate and all the net profits made through real estate are shared between the token holders, they are "losing" the extra revenues given to the team or to early investors. For example, if the bonus structure entitles certain investors to buy in with a discount of 30 percent, that means they would get a token worth 1$ of investment for just 0,7$. At the same time, a different investor may pay 1$ for the token. So, at the end, some investors pay a higher price than others for the same entitlement for revenues.

---

[1] https://www.investopedia.com/ask/answers/06/dilutivestock.asp

The Process of Security Token Offerings (STOs)

This makes sense in order to incentivize early investors for taking a higher risk with a higher dividend. Still, the bonus needs to be adequate considering the risk-revenue tradeoff. Simply speaking, the advantage given to early investors with high bonuses is given to the disadvantage of others to a certain extent. Otherwise, the offer might be very uninteresting for investors entering the fundraising round at a later stage without a discount.

The same phenomenon occurs for the *token* and the *funding distribution*.

Tokenizing real estate offers a lot of new opportunities and advantages (see the chapter *The tokenization of real estate*). But if 25 percent of the tokens are handed over to the team, advisors and similar stakeholders without investing money in return, this results in a much longer amortization period. Tokens worth 100 million Euro for example would be issued, but only 75 million Euro are invested in the form of liquid capital. In order to reach a net asset value of 100 million Euro again, probably a couple of years of reinvesting the made profits are necessary.

This example might create the impression that STOs are inefficient, however traditional real estate firms also have fees and costs. It is just more transparent when the money is raised through a STO than if the money is invested in a fund with a management fee. This is nothing that makes STOs a winning or failing concept, but still one of the major decisions within the token economics.

Funds Distribution
How is the collected money used? This reveals the approach and the way of thinking of the founders and is usually publicly

The Process of Security Token Offerings (STOs)

made available for the STO. It describes into which areas like development, human resources or marketing the money is put in. There are certain factors in which a project may require higher marketing efforts while others invest the biggest part of their money into the development. The funds distribution is interdependent with the soft cap and the hard cap. It might be that 20% of the money is spent on marketing efforts but every dollar invested after 5 million USD overall investment is delighted to marketing purposes as well – the funds distribution would change in that case.

Bonus structure
The bonus structure is intended to incentivize investors within different stages for their involvement. An earlier investment is usually characterized by a higher risk – something the investors want to see compensated with additional benefits. These benefits can be a discount or a bonus.

Additional special offers with a discount, limited in time or the investment amount, can be utilized in order to catch the attention of early investors and compensate the high risk they are taking with a possible upside.

In many projects that I have entered at a later stage, I have seen that the bonus structure has been set up by relying on an educated guess of sometimes just even one decision maker. This is shocking since the bonus structure is a very calculative element investors are looking at. Projects can dramatically loose investors due to a wrong conception of the bonus structure. If the bonus given to early investors is too low, the institutional and larger investors that usually enter at that stage will not consider it as an investment opportunity. At the same time, investors entering in later funding periods will feel they are too disadvantaged if the bonus given to previous investors is too high.

Investor rights (legally)

The investor rights need to be defined from a legal perspective. The following questions help to define the legal rights given to the token holders:

- What does the underlying asset consist of?
- Which kind of participation does the owner of a token have?
    o Monetary participation: In which ways does the token holder participate at the success of the company or a value increase of the assets?
    o Decision participation: Which voting rights are given to token holders?

- When is a participation happening? For example:

    o Dividends
        » Regular dividends
        » Dividends upon managements' decision
        » Dividends upon shareholders decision
    o Participation upon exit

- What is the lifetime of the asset?
- What is the lifetime of the issued security or the issued investor entitlements? Do certain rights expire at a given date?

The questions above are rather a guideline for the STO strategy team and help them communicating their requirements to the legal parties or departments. At the end, the definition of the investor rights and the classification as a specific asset is up to the lawyers, followed by the Regulators approval.

> **Result at the end of this step**
> The numbers are defined, and the investment vehicle is conceptualized from the financial perspective. Prospects can understand the hard facts and with the information set, specific deals can be closed.

3. Defining the stages of Fundraising

The stages of Fundraising are defined in order to match the need of money of the venture with the capital that can be acquired from investors. Stages both mean different funding rounds, known from classical Startup fundraising such as Series A and Series B, but also internal phases within one round.

For example, the venture may require 10 million Euro in the current round and wants to collect another 50 million in three years' time. Those are the **fundraising rounds**.

Within each of these fundraising rounds, there are certain *phases*. Especially for the first funding round, certain resources are necessary in order to set up the infrastructure to actually collect the money – which we herein refer to as *burn money*. When this money is collected, the basic, minimum viable infrastructure can be built in order to collect further investments. Every part of the money that is not invested into the product development or activities surrounding the actual value to be delivered, we call it *burn money*. Since there is no *direct* value created for others.

For example, the project could first collect 300.000 Euro burn money in order to build up the infrastructure to raise the money. It would then collect another 1.7 million Euro from institutional investors. When this is done and two of the ten million Euro are raised, they will actually *Go Tokenized* (in analogy to *going public* on stock markets) and offer their project to retail investors until the fundraising period is over or 10 million Euro are reached.

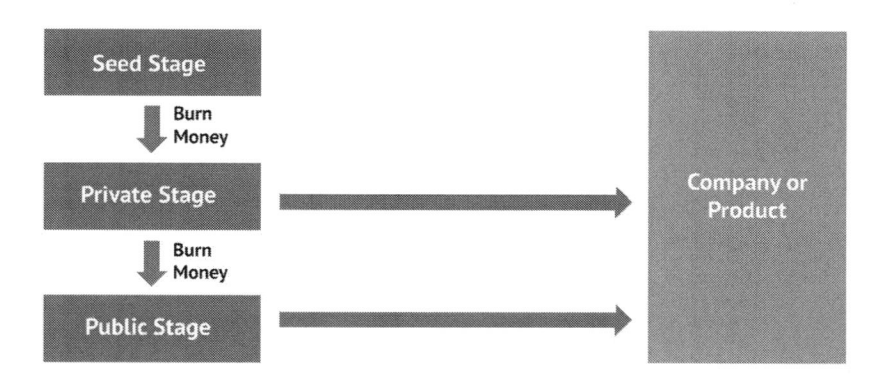

You may wonder why these three phases are necessary or why retail investors are considered in another phase. Each phase partly has the purpose of funding the next stage:

1. Seed Stage
Burn money is collected in order to prepare all relevant documents for the tokensale, set up the necessary technical infrastructure and

ensure Compliance with the respective Regulations in order to be able to collect more money from institutional investors.

At the end of this phase, the material for the token sale is prepared and the legal work is done in order to approach institutional investors.

2. Private Stage
In this stage, money that exceeds the first, minimal amount of capital needed to build the infrastructure is collected. Splitting it into two phases is necessary since it oftentimes requires more legal work than for the seed stage. The money collected in the Private stage is used for the venture itself to be financed (building the product) and a small portion of it is used to finance the legal and technical work necessary in order to enter the public stage in the next step. You may already ask why again money is collected to finance the next stage and wonder about the high dilution of invested money. Indeed, it is not always a better decision to go public. Judging by the numbers, it can be a better calculation to collect all the money during the private stage from institutional and larger investors instead of going public. Still, this is a case to case decision and other influences such as of political nature need to be taken into consideration.

3. Public Stage
The Public Stage is meant to collect money from retail investors. This requires the most legal work since different jurisdictions provide a high investor protection for individuals who cannot be classified as professional investors.

Usually, further documents and data needs to be published and certain approvals need to be obtained from the regulator. Also, the cost factor of handling many different investors shall be taken into account: More complex voting processes in the case of handing out voting rights, high costs for processing Compliance, KYC and AML process a larger group of people. This is why projects oftentimes don't even pursue the Public Stage anymore if they are able to raise all the money needed within the previous stages. Although the need of a Public Stage will be continuously re-evaluated throughout the process, the disadvantages of offering the investment to retail investors should be kept in mind. It might be a better deal at the end to agree on a bit less advantageous conditions with large investors when the public stage and the disadvantages of it can be avoided. The pros and cons of this stage will be evaluated later.

4. Defining the target investor group

In order to approach investors in the right way, the type of investors need to be demystified. The project specifies their prospects in the most accurate way, classifying them for example with the following categories:

4.1. Investor Relation Type

Which values does the investor bring into the company?

There is a general distinction between which type of resources an investor brings into the company – mainly, if the input is only of financial matters or also consists of other resources[2].

---

[2]   https://mercercapital.com/article/financial-vs-strategic-buyers/

A) **Strategic Investors**

Strategic investors not only provide money, but also other strategic benefits. That could their network of possible customers, their non-monetary resources, their experience or their reputation.

B) **Financial Investors**

These investors solely bring in money into the venture without providing further benefits. Their purpose is to buy and sell companies or shares of it. They do not buy with the intention of leveraging synergies by that[3].

4.2 Investment Purpose Type

What is the purpose of the investor when investing?

There are several terms classifying an investor regarding the purpose or the context of Investing: Institutional, retail, professional, non-professional. Some of those terms are overlapping – we will conclude the difference between institutional and retail (non-institutional) investors here since this is the differentiation that probably causes the biggest differences in approaching legal requirements.

A) **Institutional**

Institutional investors usually do investments as their main activity of business or have a larger amount of capital to invest. This is a general understanding that is spread within the financial sphere, however there are different legal considerations that investors qualify as institutional

---

[3] https://investmentbank.com/strategic-vs-financial-buyers/

or non-institutional investors. Some sources also define an institutional investor as a "person or organization that trades securities in large enough quantities that it qualifies for preferential treatment and lower fees[4]."

B) **Retail**
Non-professional investors are usually individuals who invest by the side and not to provide their major source of income by that. They invest in smaller amounts but are legally subject to higher standards of investor protection than professional investors[5].

Legal consequences
The legal considerations of the target investor group have been briefly mentioned above: Individuals are protected more strictly by Regulators, meaning that the projects are forced to provide a more standardized set of information and obtain approvals in order to offer their investment publicly to individuals.

This is why non-professional or retail investors are not relevant in certain stages of the Fundraising.

When to consider which investor?
The project should not only define which investors to target, but also the stage in which specific investors are targeted. This enables the team to provide the right information to the right

---

[4] https://www.investopedia.com/terms/i/institutionalinvestor.asp
[5] http://www.investorguide.com/article/11202/what-is-the-difference-between-retail-investors-and-institutional-investors/

people at the right time and leverage the full potential each type of investor offers.

Strategic Investors
There is an overlap between strategic and institutional investors. Almost always, a strategic investor is considered as an institutional investor already by the fact that he invests larger sums of money.

There should be a symbiose of the venture doing the Fundraising and a strategic investor in order to utilize a strategic advantage. While the venture benefits of the strategic advantages, the investor himself also is interested in investing his non-monetary resources because he benefits from the success of the venture. Hence, he can leverage his existing resources: Investing money grants him a participation at the success while he can directly influence the success by investing his other resources as well. In the best case, a WIN-WIN-WIN situation is created.

To reach this leverage of the investor's resources, he is interested in providing an amount of money that grants him a decent share or participation right of the success from the venture he is financing.

This is why strategic investors are considered early on. They invest larger amounts of money and hence mostly do not fall under the retail investor category. They can also provide guidance and strategically useful information which should be utilized from the beginning while the barrier to accept institutional investors is comparingly low.

Financial investors

The financial investors can be considered at any stage, whatsoever shall be evaluated having the option of strategic investors in mind.

Comparing *financial* with *strategic investors* can be a difficult task because you have to balance between strategic values and monetary values.

The strategic vs. monetary resources tradeoff

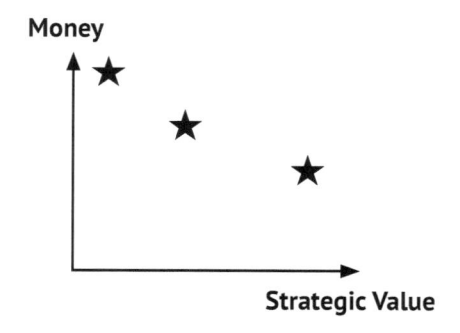

This graphic can be taken as an example when two investors offer different values for the same amount of e.g. shares in return. For 15% of the company, one of them would invest 5 million Euro and the other one would only invest 2,5 million Euro but would also offer his network of possible customers and has the benefit of giving the project a better reputation. As the graphic shows, the two dimensions *monetary value* and *strategic value* cannot directly be compared to each other. It is a subjective decision up to the project and it also depends on the phase of the Fundraising round. If the project is in urgent need of money, the monetary axis might be considered more. On the other hand, if the project has secured most of the monetary requirements, the strategic value might be better to go for.

The graphic above proves that this is a very careful decision to be taken and the advice of a domain expert might be helpful.

3. Geographical-Sociocultural

*Which Investment values and approaches
are common for an area or culture?*

The geographical type of investor outlines some of the requirements for the offering. Sociocultural aspects may reveal that some cultures are more open to risk while others try to avoid it. There are some regions where many people individually invest in shares while in other countries the ratio of people who are investing in stocks are comparingly low.

The geographical target can also enhance the market if it is the same as the (future) geographical target for customers. Raising money in the region where the project operates strengthens the local touch and may improve the reputation and the outreach or the publicity of this venture.

The sociocultural aspects are by definition rather soft factors influencing the decision than hard facts.

4. Geographical-Jurisdiction

Which legal requirements does a Regulation bring up?

The geographical target often goes hand in hand with the jurisdiction. Unless the company operates from and offers

The Process of Security Token Offerings (STOs)

to the same jurisdiction, Compliance in different jurisdictions needs to be ensured. Apparently, this makes the process a bit more complicated.

Furthermore, there are jurisdictions that over the time turned out to be more friendly to DLT and Blockchain related ventures or Fundraisings than others. However, just setting up an entity for the venture in an offshore country in order to bypass stricter Regulations in the actual country the company is targeting investors from, does not save them from complying with the respective Regulations.

During the hype of ICOs in 2017 for example, people from the United States were excluded from most of the projects and their investments were strictly prohibited by the ventures because they were afraid of facing sanctions from the United States Securities and Exchange Commission[6].

This is why investors should be selected by the jurisdiction of the country they are living in or are registered in.

> **Result at the end of this step**
> The type of investors, from *geographical, sociocultural*, the *investment purpose* and the *jurisdiction* direction are defined. The project has an overview of which investors are targeted at a specific stage of the Fundraising and can specifically approach them.

---

[6]   http://fortune.com/2019/04/05/sec-crypto-rules/

5. Adjusting the documents for investors

Having defined the target group of investors helps the project to approach them tailored to their needs and their focus. Hence, this information shall be used to adjust the documents that have been prepared in the step *Defining the business model*. For example, a family office will look at your project with a completely different perspective than an Angel Investor would do. Venture Capitalists may dive deeper into the technology behind

To match the needs and requirements of different investor types, different documents for each investor type can now be prepared. It helps to include people of the team for iterative reviews – especially the Advisory board should support this part. After having it reviewed internally, handing the documents over to people from the respective target group in order to collect more specific feedback add the cutting edge to it.

6. Dealing with secondary markets

As discussed in the general chapter about tokenization, some of the main advantages of representing assets with a token are the *transferability* and the *exchangeability*. However, getting listed on the major exchanges for digital securities requires specific action and is neither an automatic process, nor is it done by the exchanges.

Having a secondary market in place as early as possible generally lowers the risk that the token will never be tradable. Hence, it is also relevant for investors looking at the project.

Exchanges for securities are highly regulated and need to meet many standards. Therefore, also the project that wants to get the token listed on it needs to fulfil those criteria. In order to comply with them, dealing with the secondary markets is a step to take at the beginning of a Token Offering rather than at the end.

Concretely speaking, the project should first identify on which exchanges it wants to be listed. The volume, region and reputation can be relevant criteria. Now, having defined the Fundraising phases, the token economics and the investor target group, choosing the right exchanges can be done with a reasonable effort.

Then, it should reach out to every exchange and ask for the current listing criteria – this is really important in order to keep the requirements in mind when building the further structure of the token sale in the next steps.

In the best case, it is possible to get a Letter of Intent (LOI) or a similar soft commitment from the exchange that once the token is issued and it complies with the listing requirements, it can be listed on the respective exchange. This gives the project another level of trust and security.

The Process of Security Token Offerings (STOs)

> **Result at the end of this step**
> Specific exchanges to be listed on are identified and the listing requirements have been obtained. In the best case, a Letter of Intent for a listing (with the approval to publish it) is mutually signed.

7. Setting up the Banking & Finance infrastructure

At the end of the day, the project wants to collect fiat money to finance the venture or hand out their assets. Hence, the minimum infrastructure to raise money by selling a tokenized security may consist of:

- **A Banking account**
  The payments of fiat money can be received at this bank account.

- **A Custodian**
  A Custodian is "a financial institution that holds customers' securities for safekeeping in order to minimize the risk of their theft or loss[7]." An own paper about Custody can be found with the following link code.

  Link Code: 3

- **An Exchange access**
  For the case that cryptocurrencies are received, and they should be converted to fiat money, the access to an exchange,

---

[7] https://www.investopedia.com/terms/c/custodian.asp

The Process of Security Token Offerings (STOs)

a broker or an Over-The-Counter (OTC) desk should be set up where they can be liquidated.

8. Choosing the issuance platform

The issuance platform takes care of providing a technical platform on which investors can be onboarded and investments can be made. It is important to have executed the previous steps in order to choose the right STO issuance platform. It provides a user interface for prospects to register and send their money or their cryptocurrency investment to the platform, which then tracks it and makes sure the correct number of tokens is handed out to the respective investor.

There are several STO platforms that focus on different technologies, areas and regions. It needs to be chosen carefully in order to fulfil the **Compliance requirements** and the respective **data protection laws** of the countries the STO is offered to.

Not only the technical specification of the platform matters, but especially the **liquidity** it provides. There are hundreds of STO platforms available that enable projects to easily launch their token and provide the technical infrastructure to collect the investments, though many of them lack the liquidity provided by already registered investors.

> **Result at the end of this step**
> The platform for issuing the token is chosen or a clear structure about an individual software to be built exists.

9. Reaching out to Pre-STO investors

The business and the technical platform is set up and the underlying assets are defined while the legal requirements are fulfilled in order to reach out to institutional investors.

Respecting the Regulation, the tokensale can now be promoted to the investors that we already defined earlier. Most of the work is done already, so now the time has come to actually roll up the sleeves and get the hands on the phone and the email client.

If the project is legally allowed to, either a public or a private roadshow on relevant locations all over the world can be conducted to build a network of investors and showcase the project. The more investors can be convinced of the project, the better is the basis for negotiations about investments.

> **Result at the end of this step**
> The previously defined investors are contacted and regular follow ups are done. The sales process is being tracked and feedback from investors collected.

10. Choosing the type of token

In the Chapter *Token Standards*, the different types of tokens and their applicability for issuing a security token was discussed. Now, after also having defined the general setup (the token economics and the underlying asset) and the technical setup (the issuance platform), these requirements can be translated into a specific type of token.

The criteria for choosing a token type are:

A) The issuance platform. It might already edict a token standard to use or limit the options.

B) The legal force. The functionalities of the token must be restrictive enough to comply with the Regulation.

C) The requirements to offer investors the underlying asset. The token standard must provide the right functions to implement the investors entitlements or at least be adjustable in that way

> **Result at the end of this step**
>
> A specific token standard has been chosen and further enhancements that may be required are defined, so that the development team can implement them simultaneously.

11. Preparing the legal setup for the Pre-STO round(s)

The Pre-STO round is the first time money of external people is being invested, apart from so-called FFF (friends, family and fools) investors. Hence, it is important to have the legal setup in place, meaning
- Agreements to sell tokens
- Necessary incorporations of legal entities
- Necessary licenses and approvals

There are certain templates for agreements for token sales that have been previously used by other projects. However, they do not replace a legal consultation by a lawyer.

> **Result at the end of this step**
>
> All legal documents are ready to be signed, the last approvals are obtained and the project is allowed to receive money from investors for giving out certain (representations or entitlements for) assets in return.

12. Running the Pre-STO rounds

All the initial setup is done to close the deals: The investors that were approached and want to invest can now sign a binding contract for their investment. After having the investments secured by a signature, the money should actually be collected in a short period of time and in a liquid form – either in the form of fiat money or cryptocurrencies. Since the project's expenses are occurring in fiat money form, this way is easier to handle. If cryptocurrencies are collected, it is up to the project whether they are converted to fiat money right away or they are held as cryptocurrencies in the wallet.

Most of the steps done within the Pre-STO round are project specific, e.g. the marketing. Hence, for this step and it's presentation a couple of strategy meetings in which the Advisory Board is included, shall be held.

> **Result at the end of this step**
>
> The company collected a sufficient amount of money in order to cover the expenses to build the STO and reach out to (retail) investors.

13. Redefining the STO strategy

This phase is rather a continuous and iterative one than a step that is only executed once. Especially during the Pre-STO stage, it is important to keep the strategy updated with new available information.

The following questions shall be answered:

1) Is a Public Sale necessary?
As mentioned earlier, offering the project to retail investors brings up much higher requirements both technically and legally than for institutional investors. If the project collects more money than expected during the Pre-STO, it might be better off by not performing a public sale because the potential of additional money collected does not justify the additional effort.

2) Do we need to adjust the roadmap?
The roadmap both for the tokensale itself, as well as for the overall project might be required to be changed. If the Pre-STO phase took more time than expected, that may cause a delay for the offering to retail investors and maybe also to the technical roadmap for the product development if the tokenized assets are startup shares.

3) Do we need to adjust the bonus structure?
The bonus structure has the main intention of creating a buzz around the project early on and incentivize investors taking higher risk with a higher bonus. The new information from the Pre-STO round might lead to a different estimation for a fair bonus structure. One of the risks that

The Process of Security Token Offerings (STOs)

a Crowdfunding project has is to not reach the Soft Cap and hence needing to return the left portion of the money.

> **Result at the end of this step**
> The strategy is redefined, covering the information gathered throughout the Pre-STO and can be broken down into concrete steps to execute the STO itself.

If the Soft Cap has already been reached during the Pre-STO, this risk does not exist for future investors anymore – so it might not be necessary to incentivize them as much as before anymore.

14. Preparing the technical setup for a public tokensale

Depending on the step *Choosing the issuance platform*, further implementations might be necessary. Especially the different payment channels need to be implemented consistently.

When cryptocurrencies are accepted as an investment, they can be processed automatically. It has to be ensured that payments are handled correctly when the STO is oversubscribed (the demand is higher than the actual supply of tokens). While cryptocurrencies can be processed automatically, payments in Euros or Dollar cannot. If a larger investor buys the last shares of a company, this information must be processed manually but fast in order to block further cryptocurrency investments that the Smart Contract otherwise would accept. This is a very technical challenge that we are not going to elaborate further.

The Process of Security Token Offerings (STOs)

Cryptocurrency payments
The advantages of cryptocurrency payments are:
- They could be processed with lower transaction costs
- The payments can be highly automated without including a lot of stakeholders or implementing complex processes

The disadvantages of cryptocurrency payments are:
- Cryptocurrencies alone might only be accessible for tech-savvy investors
- Custody can be a legal challenge
- There is no centralized party who can recover lost funds [8]

Fiat money payments
Fiat money means all the currencies issued by central banks like US-Dollar and Euro.
The advantages of fiat money payments are:
- People are used to it
- No conversion is necessary (only between fiat currencies)
- Less risk of price fluctuation since the money is received in the form it is needed in

The disadvantages of cryptocurrency payments are:
- Probably higher handling fees
- More complex to accept payments from different regions

---

[8] Wasn't this the initial idea of cryptocurrencies? Yes! However, this is a tradeoff everybody individually has to decide about. On the one hand you may want to use decentralized technology (in this case cryptocurrencies), on the other hand there are also examples where projects lost their money due to human errors when using cryptocurrencies - that could have been prevented by utilizing a centralized Custodian.

The Process of Security Token Offerings (STOs)

What's the best payment method?
It all depends on the target group. If the target group of investors consists of only Blockchain enthusiasts and cryptocurrency users, focusing on cryptocurrencies might be a viable approach. This is very unlikely in reality, hence accepting both types of currencies, fiat and crypto, is usually the best.

The interoperability has to be ensured from the very beginning in order to correctly process both payment streams simultaneously.

The larger investments in early phases such as the Pre-STO round are typically done with fiat money. This is why we are setting up the payment processes after the Pre-STO round. As long as only fiat money is accepted, inconsistencies between both payment streams are not existent. And following a lean approach, we only set up the payment processes for cryptocurrencies when we decided that we want to target retail investors and allow them to invest in cryptocurrencies, considering the new information after the Pre-STO round.

> **Result at the end of this step**
> The portal is set up in a test environment, so that users possibly could sign up, reserve tokens and invest for test purposes with payment gateways already integrated.

15. Integrating Know-Your-Customer and Anti-Money-Laundering processes

You might wonder why dealing with KYC and AML requirements is done in one of the last steps. Indeed, KYC and AML requirements shall already be taken into account when the issuance platform is chosen. But by adding certain payment methods on top and eventually integrating more third-party providers, the whole infrastructure needs to be consistently aligned so that whichever path the user follows from the website to the investment, the respective necessary measures are implemented.

> **Result at the end of this step**
> The portal applies certain measures to ensure KYC and AML compliance. Investors can go through the KYC process and get approved. When money is received, it is ensured that money laundering is not possible.

16. Auditing the technical infrastructure

Four eyes see more than two and six more than four. Accepting (cryptocurrency) payments requires high security standards. Especially, but not only, when individual software is used, an audit should be made - likely independent from the developers and their interests. Hence, including a third-party to audit the Smart Contracts and the tokensale infrastructure is a common practice.

The more peer reviews that are done, the better the security probably gets in order to provide investors an easy-to-use and secure way of investing into the project.

The Process of Security Token Offerings (STOs)

The Auditor shall take the responsibility to check whether the infrastructure meets certain (legal) security requirements and is able to process investments consistently.

It is better to spend a little money on the Audit instead of risking to spend a lot of money afterwards when done wrong.

> **Result at the end of this step**
> The portal is set up, tested, and audited. The investor can register, go through the KYC process by providing his documents and can invest – AML measures are implemented.

17. Running the public tokensale

The time has come to get investors on the tokensale that has now been prepared for weeks or months.

The technical setup has to be brought into the live stage, so that investors can sign up. At the same time, all the marketing activities for the tokensale can be rolled out.

Additional staff is starting their work in order to support the investor requests during the tokensale period and after.

Although most of the processes are automated, the core team should have an eye on what is happening. The transactions may be reviewed manually by the support team and numbers verified once in a while. Both the fiat money and the cryptocurrency stream must be monitored so the doors will be shut when the hardcap is reached.

The Process of Security Token Offerings (STOs)

If the received cryptocurrencies are instantly converted into fiat money, this automated conversion shall be monitored as well.

At the end, all data should be peer-reviewed **before** *any* token is given out.

> **Result at the end of this step**
>
> The money is collected and, presumably, the soft cap or even the hard cap is reached. The money is held by the Custodians and investors are waiting to receive their tokens.

18. Post-STO work and managing the money

The tokens are now handed out to the investors when all KYC and AML requirements are met, and the investor is entitled to receive the tokens on the wallet. These transactions shall be documented with all the data although they are stored on the Blockchain.

Further Accounting procedures give an overview about the overall expenses the STO brought up, the money that is available to the startup or for the underlying assets. Investor Relations are starting to begin.

> **Result at the end of this step**
>
> The venture is ready to operate within their regular business and utilize the new resources.

The Process of Security Token Offerings (STOs)

Summary

It is important to consider the activities of a token sale at the right time. The 18 step process provides an idea of how a token sale can look like.

1. Defining the business model
2. Defining the token use-case (ICO) or the token structure (STO)
3. Defining the stages of Fundraising
4. Defining the target investor group
5. Adjusting the documents for investors
6. Dealing with secondary markets
7. Setting up the Banking & Finance infrastructure
8. Choosing the issuing platform
9. Reaching out to Pre-STO investors
10. Choosing the type of token
11. Preparing the legal setup for the Pre-STO round(s)
12. Running the Pre-STO rounds
13. Redefining the STO strategy
14. Preparing the technical setup for a public tokensale
15. Integrating Know-Your-Customer and Anti-Money-Laundering processes
16. Auditing the technical infrastructure
17. Running the public tokensale
18. Post-STO work and managing the money

The Process of Security Token Offerings (STOs)

Blockchain Platforms for tokenization

As the previous chapter depicted, tokens can be deployed on different Blockchains. This is not to be confused with the issuance platforms that provide an interface to issue tokens on a *specific* Blockchain.

General considerations

There is no *single* or *the* Blockchain. The Blockchain itself is a concept and has many different implementations. Hence, when issuing a tokenized security, we are in most regards free to choose the right Blockchain to build the token on. Every Blockchain has its own advantages and disadvantages.

The trade-off between different Blockchains or distributed ledgers

Usually, Blockchain (platforms) each offer a different tradeoff between the following dimensions:

- Decentralization
- Speed & Costs
- Security

Decentralization

Blockchain Trade-Off

Speed & Costs   **Security**

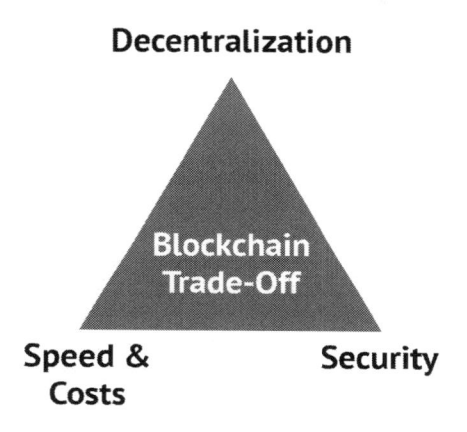

Why is it a tradeoff?
The three dimensions are sometimes contradictive to each other[1]. For example, *speed* and *decentralization* can only be achieved together to a certain extend. Including many parties to run the network would increase the decentralization of it, while the speed might decrease.

The most well-known trade-off lies between *security* and *speed*.

Apart from Blockchain, we can relate to a general security vs. convenience trade-off in many ways:

---

[1] https://www.research.ed.ac.uk/portal/en/publications/speedsecurity-tradeoffs-in-blockchain-protocols(141c78de-df5e-4afe-ab82-1cf81039e7dc).html

1. Having a 32-digit password is probably much *safer* than a 4-digit one, but far less *convenient*

2. Driving the car at 120km/h is probably less *secure* than riding it at 80km/h, but *faster*

3. Riding the bicycle with a helmet is probably far less *convenient* than without, but probably much *safer* than without.

The same counts for a Blockchain: More complex hash algorithms, higher decentralization and a larger network may add another level to the security while it decreases the speed.

Hence, speaking of a trade-off, we cannot enjoy the maximum of each dimension. We rather have to choose the approach or the trade-off that serves our specific use-case best. This is why there is no single go-to Blockchain platform that shall be used for every type of (security) token issuance. Many influences such as the technical requirements, the type of investors and several others shall be taken into account when selecting the right platform to issue a security token. At the same time, specific Blockchain platforms or issuance platforms would apparently sell their solution as the best one to you. An experienced Advisor knows the differences, as well as the advantages and disadvantages, of the projects.

Different Blockchain Platforms in comparison

As depicted above, every Blockchain or DLT platform has it's own advantages and disadvantages. Hence, we will look at the popular platforms from the perspective of a token issuer. This perspective can be very different from others since launching a security token and making it tradable brings up quite different requirements than a cryptocurrency or other applications have.

Ethereum
Ethereum is the far most popular and often used platform to issue any kind of token – which does not necessarily mean that it is also the best platform to choose for any type of token. Whatsoever, the popularity and the positive network effects resulting out of that cannot be neglected. Having many tokens deployed on the Ethereum Blockchain makes it more likely for service providers to enter that space and create a rich ecosystem of digital securities services on Ethereum, the same goes vice versa. And this is exactly what can be found out with a non-empirical research: Many security token platforms, secondary markets, standards, users, investors and projects surround Ethereum. Ethereum has been built since August 2014 and therefore has surpassed a comparingly long history of development and testing.

Coming to the hard facts, Ethereum is less scalable than other platforms such as EOS. The transaction costs are reasonable, but not cheap. At the time of writing, they amount ca. 0,10 USD[2]. Taking into account that using a decentralized exchange would in most cases still be cheaper than the fees paid to a bank when selling e.g. a stock, this sounds like a negligible amount of money. However, Ethereum is quite expensive compared to other platforms and the scalability is limited. If this doesn't change, Ethereum might be outperformed by other platforms in the long run. The network

---

[2] https://bitinfocharts.com/comparison/ethereum-transactionfees.html

Blockchain Platforms for tokenization

effects Ethereum possesses in a good way whatsoever would cause this transition taking a long time since people would move from Ethereum to other distributed ledgers or Blockchain. Ethereum uses an own programming language called Solidity, which limits the amount of developers that are familiar with it. Overall, Ethereum as a public Blockchain is the most popular one to issue tokens on.

Hyperledger Fabric
Hyperledger is hosted by the Linux Foundation and has a solid team of developers. It proclaims itself as an "enterprise grade, open source distributed ledger framework".

Hyperledger embraces several projects, but *Hyperledger Fabric* is the far-most popular and run by IBM[3] and hence most people know the Fabric version of it.

What is interesting in Hyperledger concerning security tokens is the FabToken. It is a token management system to deploy and use tokens with the functionality that is needed. Users can be identified, but the parties of a transaction are not revealed to everyone. The FabToken is also interoperable with Smart Contracts written on Ethereum. Meaning that the large network effects and the popularity that Ethereum has, concerning the adoption by users, can be leveraged while using Hyperledger Fabric as the technical platform[4].

---

[3] https://www.ibm.com/blogs/blockchain/2018/08/hyperledger-fabric-what-you-need-to-know-about-the-framework-that-powers-ibm-blockchain/

[4] https://www.linkedin.com/pulse/token-hyperledger-fabric-andy-martin

Blockchain Platforms for tokenization

An interesting move in the regard to security tokens was made when a security tokenization project joined Hyperledger[5] for an acceleration program.

The Smart Contracts can be written in popular programming languages such as Go or Java which opens it to a wide pool of developers that are already familiar with those technologies. Along with the Ethereum interoperability, Hyperledger Fabric provides a well thought-through platform covering aspects like identity and privacy while also being adaptable by issuers, developers and users or investors.

EOS
EOS is a platform for the development of decentralized applications. It is supposed to have a high transaction throughput while ensuring low transaction costs. The platform provides certain technical advantages compared to other platforms, e.g. the fact it is designed for Inter Blockchain Communication[6]. Hence, a token deployed on the EOS network may also be integrated into other Blockchains. Some token standards based on EOS are interoperable with Ethereum based standards – they can be exchanged without the need of any third-party like an exchange to intervene. Specifically important within the context of security tokens are the Hierarchical Role Based Permissions. Having a role system directly integrated within the platform makes the establishment of a security token framework much more feasible.

---

[5] https://thetokenist.io/securitize-others-join-hyperledger-blockchain-project/
[6] https://github.com/EOSIO/eos

Security tokens on EOS[7]

A special Financial Securities Protocol has been released in order to unify the way tokenized securities can be launched within EOS. This protocol consists of five different modules:

A) Security
Basic functionality of a financial asset.

B) Regulator
Restrictions to ensure Compliance for the security token, e.g. by preventing users from sending the token to a non-verified wallet address.

C) Exchange
Exchange that can be implemented as a limit order book or as a one-way liquidity provider[8].

D) Registry
KYC and AML procedures to map EOS accounts with real-world identities.

E) Communication
Exchange of information between the securities protocol and external stakeholders.

---

[7] https://github.com/fspnetwork/fsp-core/raw/master/whitepaper/Financial_Securities_Protocol.pdf
[8] https://medium.com/fspnetwork/introducing-financial-securities-protocol-9d21bd66a0f8

R3 Corda

Corda is the Blockchain platform developed by the company R3, hence often referenced as R3 Corda. Since Corda is branding itself as an enterprise Blockchain platform, it has a very different approach than public Blockchains like Ethereum or EOS. Corda is rather focused on specific enterprises that integrate the platform into their business operations to interact with each other on a trustworthy Blockchain platform without intermediaries ensuring this trustworthiness.

Hence, these enterprises in terms of security tokens could be the exchanges, the offering platforms, the issuer and eventually other service providers involved. It strengthens the privacy and identity standards – anonymity like it exists on other platforms is not wanted within most of the use-cases, especially when dealing with securities. Instead, the parties interacting with each other shall be identified and transparent[9]. This makes Corda an interesting platform in the regard to security tokens that are strictly regulated and require identification processes by nature in order to prevent money laundering and criminal activities. Another advantage in the realm of securities settlements that Corda claims to possess is the settlement finality[10] – meaning that settled transactions should be permanently stored and not subject to "blockchain reorganiations" that could cause issues[11].

---

[9] https://www.r3.com/wp-content/uploads/2019/01/R3-Quick-Facts.pdf
[10] https://ec.europa.eu/info/business-economy-euro/banking-and-finance/financial-markets/post-trade-services/settlement-finality_en
[11] https://medium.com/corda/asset-tokenisation-an-idea-whose-time-has-come-but-not-for-the-reasons-you-might-expect-ac4d0feab9e1

Blockchain Platforms for tokenization

An advantage of Corda is that apart from Smart Contracts, they semantically support *Smart **Legal** Contracts*[12] as well in legal prose. The Smart Contracts can be written in popular programming languages such as *Kotlin* or *Java* which opens it to a wide pool of developers that are already familiar with those technologies.

Waves

The Waves platform is an open-source Blockchain platform. Waves describes itself as a solution for the Web3.0 – a decentralized form of the web we know. Waves entered the space of security tokens much later than the other popular Blockchain platforms like Ethereum. Hence, the news and the vibe around Waves in this regard is very calm. However, they recently announced their tokenization platform[13]. At the same time, a decentralized and regulated exchange shall be provided in order to trade the tokens deployed on the Security Token Issuance Platform (STIP)[14]. This exchange whatsoever does not seem to be regulated for security tokens, but rather for *Virtual Financial Assets* that are regulated on Malta.

What sets it apart from the other Blockchains is that the issuance platform is directly enhanced by Waves and should provide users with a clickable interface, enabling them to launch a STO without any programming knowledge. In the case of Ethereum, many issuance platforms exist on the market – but the ties between the issuance platform and the core Waves platform seem much stronger than the ones between Ethereum and its third-party platforms.

[12] https://docs.corda.net/releases/release-M1.0/tutorial-contract.html
[13] https://tokenomica.com
[14] https://tokenomica.com

& The Process of Security Token Offerings (STOs)

Token Standards

As we defined earlier, a token from a business perspective can be seen as a digital unit stored on a Blockchain in order to represent certain rights or the (partial) ownership of an asset. In order to achieve these goals, a worldwide community works on different standards for tokens. Depending on the Blockchain platform, different standards and technical features are available.

Technically, a token can be implemented freely by the issuer. However, having a different token implementation for every asset makes the issuance complicated since secondary markets, user applications and any other interface would need to adopt this implementation to integrate those tokens. There is no single standard for security tokens yet established, whatsoever there are a few proposals that can be found and are starting to be adopted.

We will first discuss the purpose and the requirements of a token standard and then give a very brief overview of the current token standards that are being developed, mainly on the Ethereum Blockchain since it has the biggest relevance within the market and token standards from other Blockchains try to be compatible to those as well in order to ensure interoperability.

The requirements of an asset-backed token

Technically speaking, a token is nothing more than a unit stored on a Blockchain with certain *functions*. Since it consists of *functions* and not only of *states*, people used the term *programmable money* for it. Every function is a piece of code on the Blockchain that can be executed by one or more parties. So, which functions shall a token have in order to serve as a digital representation of an asset?

Most important is the *transfer* function. This might look very obvious since handing over cash is also a form of a transfer function. A normal transfer function of a cryptocurrency or a utility token only checks if the sender of a transaction has sufficient funds, subtracts the transaction amount from the senders account and adds it to the receivers account. In this case, the sender of the money or the cryptocurrency would *call (trigger the execution of)* the transfer function: The intervention of the receiver is not needed.

It gets a bit more complicated when we deal with securities: Compliance has to be ensured and securities shall not be transferable to unknown addresses within a network. Hence, we need further security measures directly implemented into a token or specifically into the transfer method. For example, the transfer method shall not always transfer the money immediately, but first validate if the receiver is entitled to receive those tokens – for example that he is not a terrorist. This aspect depicts the biggest difference between utility and security tokens. Most of the other functions of utility and security tokens are similar, e.g. a function that enables third-parties to read the balance of a certain wallet address. Unlike utility tokens who follow the decentralized idea of a Blockchain and therefore do not enable fund recoveries (you can only access the funds when you possess the private key), security tokens are believed to have recovery methods and come with many more restrictions.

Token Standardization

As discussed within initiatives around security tokens, a security token standard shall fulfill the certain requirements:

A security token **MUST**:
- Have a function for transfers that also can be asked if the transfer was successful and if not, returns a reason why it failed
- Be able to force a token transfer when legal action requires to do so, or funds have to be recovered
- Be able to insert data that is not accessed on the Blockchain, but originated by a third-party source, into the meta data of a token transfer apart from the data on the Blockchain
- emit standard events for issuance and redemption
- require signed data to be passed into a transfer transaction in order to validate it on-chain
- "Be able to attach metadata to a subset of a token holder's balance such as special shareholder rights or data for transfer restrictions[1]"
- "support querying and subscribing to updates on any relevant documentation for the security[2]"

---

[1] https://github.com/ethereum/EIPs/issues/1411
[2] https://github.com/ethereum/EIPs/issues/1411

A security token **SHOULD**:
- be compatible to the standard implementation *ERC20* and *ERC777*.

A security token **SHOULD NOT**:
- restrict the range of asset classes across jurisdictions which can be represented.

Most of the security token standards that are being discussed focus on the implementation on a specific Blockchain (platform). As you can see, in the above requirements the ERC20 and ERC777 are mentioned which are based on the Ethereum Blockchain.

We will briefly explain the most relevant Ethereum token standards respecting the relevance for the issuance of tokenized securities.

General Ethereum token standards

ERC-20
ERC-20 is the most popular token standard on the Ethereum Blockchain. At the time of writing, more than 180,000 different tokens are deployed on Ethereum[3].

ERC-20 is the simplest form of an Ethereum token, consisting of simple functions for transfers, checking the token balance and a few variables. It consists of no more than six functions that are described in the appendix (or under the link code below). With those functions, simple transfers can be made, and Smart Contracts

---

[3]   https://etherscan.io/tokens

Token Standards

can be given the allowance to withdraw a specified amount of tokens from a certain wallet.

Link Code: 4

ERC-223

The ERC-223 standard was invented as an improved version of ERC-20 token and therefore can be understood as a specialized version of it. Due to the simplicity of the ERC-20 implementation and the incautious behavior of the users, tokens worth several million USD were lost.

For example, some Smart Contracts cannot receive tokens. While a Smart Contract for real estate investments expects you to send a certain number of tokens to it as an investment, there are certain Smart Contracts that don't. For example, a Smart Contract that handles the logistics process between two parties: It only manages different states like *"order received"*, *"order processed"*, *"delivery started"* and *"delivery completed"*. If someone now sends tokens to this Smart Contract, they will be lost. Imagine it like a vending machine that only accepts credit cards and you insert a dollar bill – the machine simply has no function to react to that and the money will be stuck inside forever. The Smart Contract similarly does not implement a function that processes those tokens that were being sent to it. At the same time, by using the ERC-20 standard, the transfer still would have happened, and the tokens would be unrecoverably locked within this Smart Contract. Since the Smart Contract also cannot be changed by any person afterwards, there is also no way of manually restoring the tokens. The vending machine might be opened by the vending machine operator, but the Blockchain has no centralized operator and hence nobody can *open* it to get the tokens back. Although this seems like a very rare occasion to occur, many people lost a lot of money due to small mistakes like sending their tokens to the wrong Smart Contract.

ERC-223 shall solve this issue by not allowing token transfers to Smart Contracts that don't support token receiving.

As also mentioned within the ERC-20 description, there is a difference for the user when he sends tokens to another user by the *transfer* method or to a Smart Contract by using the *transferFrom* method. Now, with ERC-223, the user does not need to worry or think about whether he send the tokens to a Smart Contract or a user. All is combined within the *transfer* method. If a token the Smart Contract generally cannot handle this token transfer, the transaction is being rejected – without locking funds.

How relevant is ERC-223?
Since the ERC-223 standard solves general issues of the ERC-20 standard, it would be the best way to go for most of the cases. It is really rare that an ERC-20 token is the better approach than ERC-223 to implement a token.

ERC-20 whatsoever was the first popular standard and is therefore often referenced – it is also used as a subsidizing term since ERC-223 technically is also a derived version from ERC-20.

Token Standards

ERC-777[4]

This token standard claims to be another improvement of the ERC-20 version. So called operators are able to send tokens on behalf of another address with ERC-777. The same goes for notifying the system about these transactions (so-called send/receive hooks in technical terms).

Side note: Fungible and Non-Fungible tokens

There is a general distinction between fungible and non-fungible tokens. Above, we spoke about fungible tokens, meaning tokens of which every unit is equal[5]. Imagine it like a cinema ticket that is not personalized. If you and your friend buy two tickets, it does not matter with which ticket you are entering. The employee of the cinema simply checks if you have *one* ticket. The tickets are hence **fungible**, one is like the other.

The opposite are **non-fungible** tokens where every unit is unique. This could be a driver's license or an annual ticket for the public transport that is personalized. The police man checks that the driver's license you handed over to him is actually yours. One driving license is not like the other.

Speaking of tokens, the driver's license token would be a non-fungible token and the cinema ticket would be a fungible token.

---

[4] https://eips.ethereum.org/EIPS/eip-777
[5] https://medium.com/altcoin-magazine/non-fungible-tokens-from-a-legal-perspective-51de03ea0b06

Token Standards

For the cases we are dealing with, this distinction is not directly necessary, but this is an important thing to know when comparing token standards and hearing of fungible or non-fungible tokens.

ERC-721[6]
This is the main standard for non-fungible tokens on Ethereum.

A very brief overview of the three most-relevant and general token standards

Token Standard	Purpose
ERC-20	Simple standard token
ERC-223	Improved version of ERC-20 to minimize losses
ERC-777	Different token transfer functions to send tokens on behalf of others and send/receive hooks
ERC-721	Non-Fungible token standard

These are the general standards for any kind of token.

Standards specifically for security tokens on Ethereum

Ethereum also offers specific token standards for security tokens.

ERC-1404: Simple Restricted Token Standard[7]
ERC-20 is a very open standard that does not semantically include restrictions for token transfers. Since securities laws might require certain actions or restrictions to be integrated, ERC-1404 allows that from it's core.

---

[6] http://erc721.org
[7] https://github.com/ethereum/EIPs/issues/1404

Token Standards

For example, you may want to restrict the token transfers in order that tokens can only be received by people who were successfully identified before. The key differences between the ERC-1404 standard specialized on securities and the abstract ERC-20 lie in between the transfer restrictions and the interface to query the reason when a transaction was rejected. It includes a human-readable explanation that can be accessed from the Smart Contract.

By design, the standard is backwards compatible with ERC-20 since it only adds functionality on top but does not remove the essentials of it.

ERC-1400: Security Token Standard

The ERC-1400 is a set of different standard interfaces for security tokens on the Ethereum Blockchain. Interfaces in their meaning for programming refer to the need that a specific implementation requires a defined set of functionalities. Hence, if a specific standard is used, the code automatically ensures that the token that is being created actually embraces all the functions it is supposed to according to the standard. The standards generally should be backwards compatible with ERC-20 and easily extended to be compatible with ERC-777[8].

All the following ERC standards are part of the ERC-1400 family:
- ERC-1594
- ERC-1410
- ERC-1643
- ERC-1644

---

[8] https://github.com/ethereum/EIPs/issues/1411

Token Standards

ERC-1594: Core Security Token Standard[9]

ERC-1594 provides the core standard for security tokens. Core in this case means that ERC-1594 provides the core and basic functionality; other functionality is being added in further standards or on an individual basis. It embraces error signaling, off-chain data injection and issuance / redemption.

ERC-1410: Partially Fungible Token Standard[10]

When tokens are enriched with further functionality, apart from just being used as a matter of record keeping, further meta data may have to be stored with them. This again requires that the tokens need to be (partially) fungible – meaning that token A can be distinguished from token B. This is not always necessary but depending on the functionality that is added to the token, might be required. In this case, ERC-1410 provides the corresponding interface for that.

ERC-1643: Document Management Standard[11]

This token standard allows documents stored elsewhere to be attached directly to a token. Hence, further legal documents that are not stored in a programmable format, but for example in a scanned document file, can be attached.

ERC-1644: Controller Token Operation Standard[12]

This token standard allows forced transfers, hence the issuer, acting as a controller, can manually execute transfers in order to

---

[9] https://github.com/ethereum/EIPs/issues/1594
[10] https://github.com/ethereum/EIPs/issues/1410
[11] https://github.com/ethereum/EIPs/issues/1643
[12] https://github.com/ethereum/EIPs/issues/1644

comply with regulatory requirements or when he has been forced himself to do so.

Summary: Security Token Standards

A token standard aims to provide a unified interface for the implementation of tokens, so that stakeholders can easily integrate them into their infrastructure. The Ethereum token standards can be split up into general token standards and security token standards. The security token standards are dominated by the ERC-1400 category that most token standards fall under, however the ERC-1404 serves as a simplistic token standard for security tokens.

Standard	Categorized under	Description
ERC-1400	none	General Security Token Standard and root category of the specific standards
ERC-1594	ERC-1400	Core Security Token Standard
ERC-1410	ERC-1400	Partially Fungible Token Standard
ERC-1643	ERC-1400	Document Management Standard
ERC-1644	ERC-1400	Controller Token Operation Standard
ERC-1404	none	Simple Restricted Token Standard

The Process of Security Token Offerings (STOs)

Regulation of Security Token Offerings (STOs)

One of the advantages of tokenizing assets is that it can be done in an automated way, with reusable frameworks and templates for every matter. One asset after the other can be tokenized within seconds - this is the *vision*. However, while the technical standards and implementations are developed very fast and hence offer wide possibilities for automation, the legal parts are far from being established. Blockchains and Security tokens are a new phenomenon which one might call difficult to fit into the existing laws. Regulations in that field are very volatile, and many settings depend on the specific project.

However, being compliant with the applicable Regulations is the only way to act on a legal ground and be successful in the long run.

It might sound like having very tight and pre-defined boundaries that a Security Token Offering has to fit in. In reality, there are many variables to be filled and many different options to choose from. For example, both the jurisdiction where the company is incorporated and the jurisdiction where investors are targeted from matters. Hence, choosing the jurisdiction to incorporate in wisely can be advantageous in terms of freedom of choice, costs, efficiency, speed, reputation or taxes.

This chapter shall convey a basic overview about relevant Regulations, general terms explained for non-lawyers and then draw a comparative analysis of different jurisdictions with their advantages and disadvantages.

In order to decide about a jurisdiction to be chosen, further research has to be made and this is no legal advice.

Securities vs. everything that is not a security
Issuing securities or financial instruments brings certain regulatory requirements with it. The purpose of tokenizing an asset and offering it to the public is simply to raise money by giving out these securities in return – oftentimes company shares (equity) or participation rights for dividends or revenues.

As described in the chapter The *ICO wild west*, people who issued utility tokens tried to avoid falling under any financial Regulation. Many have been fooled into believing that merely by *classifying* their token as a utility, they could avoid having to follow specific security rules[1].

It might be possible to pave the way accordingly so that the issued token does not classify as a security. However, implementing a utility token that does not provide a utility does not make any sense and led to massive losses of token values in the past. In most of the cases, the nature of the project indicates

---

[1] Maas, Thijs – Initital Coin Offerings: When Are tokens Securities in the EU and US?, 2019, p. 22

Regulation of Security Token Offerings (STOs)

whether a utility or a security is being issued rather than being a free decision to be taken.

In the following we will solely concentrate on security tokens.

While there is an active discussion about utility tokens being regulated as securities or not, the case of security tokens is quite clear - by utilizing a security token, projects by nature **pursue their activity to be regulated as an offering of securities**. In order to keep this topic simple and understandable, a short case study with the persona Bill is integrated to illustrate the topic.

Scenario

> Bill has a great idea for a startup and has worked on the supply chain solution he has in mind for a year. He decides to raise money and wants to give away shares of the company in return. Doing that in the traditional world requires a massive amount of paperwork since he wants to include many investors that shall be able to trade their assets. He has heard that security tokens shall simplify this process and make it leaner. Hence, he decides to issue a token that is considered as a security, specifically as an equity like security.

The main question is:
What makes a security token a security token?

It depends on the perspective or the starting point:
1) "We implement a security token (*technically*), so it falls under financial Regulation *XYZ* (*legally*)"

   technical conception ➜ *(leads to)* ➜ *legal classification*

Regulation of Security Token Offerings (STOs)

2) "We issue a security under financial Regulation XYZ (legally), so it is implemented as a security token (technically)"

legal construct ➜ *(leads to)* ➜ *technical implementation*

What varies is the perspective you are coming from: Either by starting with the legal framework and consideration bringing up certain requirements that then can be implemented technically. Or, the other way around, coming from the technical perspective of implementing a token and based on the implementation the token is classified as a security or not.

It is obvious that in most of the cases the issuer purposely wants to issue a security (token) and therefore would start with the legal perspective. The overall goal shall be to raise money with a specific setup and legal composition – the implementation in forms of a security token is just one of the vehicles or implementations to reach that goal. For example, the issuer's goal would be to give out shares of the company. The legal object would be a share. The technology whatsoever can be a token stored on the Blockchain, but also just a normal paper.

> Bill started with the aim of raising money for his startup and broke it down into giving out equity. He came from the legal construct and then decides to issue a "tokenized security".

The term 'security' of a security token causes the application of security laws in many jurisdictions. But the classification as a (subcategory of) security tokens also does not imply that this

Regulation of Security Token Offerings (STOs)

token is necessarily characterized as a security under securities law.

Putting the aspects mentioned above simply:
- Calling a token a utility token does not automatically make it a utility token
- Calling a token a security token could cause the application of security laws
- The classification as a (subcategory of) security tokens also does not imply that this token is necessarily characterized as a security under securities law
- Imposed compliance requirements can constitute legal burdens for token issuers[2]

This might look very confusing at the beginning, so we are going to dive into these requirements a bit deeper.

> Bill has decided to issue a "security". He consequently decides to issue a regulated security that has to follow e.g. the securities law.

Requirements for the issuer of Security Tokens

Generally speaking, laws follow two major goals in the field of security tokens:

A) Protecting investors

B) Prevent fraudulent activities and money laundering

---

[2] Maas, Thijs – Initital Coin Offerings: When Are tokens Securities in the EU and US?, 2019, p. 23

Those are the two main objectives that can be found independent from the concrete implementation in almost every jurisdiction. *How* a jurisdiction answers them is different. Depending on that, it results into certain requirements for the issuer. This is why some jurisdictions may be considered advantageous against others for specific activities.

Protecting investors
This is done by restricting the offers that companies can make to other people and companies, hoping to sort out all activities that are not trustworthy and only allowing companies to deal with money of other people when they can prove to have serious objectives and not intend to act on a fraudulent ground.

This can happen in the form of requiring the publication of certain documents, licenses or monetary backups from the project.

Prevent fraudulent activities and money laundering
While it is of high interest to protect investors from being scammed by companies, it is also of high interest of a jurisdiction that money laundering by investors is prohibited. If no *Anti Money Laundering* (AML) measures are developed, criminals could launder or wash their money through a token sale. Money that was handed around within criminal activities could then by reinvested and then withdrawn under the cover of this investment.

Anti Money Laundering is highly related to Know Your Customer (KYC) processes which aim to identify the investor and thereby detect suspicious activities.

> Bill is preparing for selling the securities in Germany. Since Germany is an EU country, the Anti Money Laundering Directive[3] of the EU shall apply. Hence, Bill implements a KYC process in which every investor has to register, enter his address and his personal credentials and then has to verify the correctness of the submitted data in a video call. Bill uses a third-party to check whether a registered person has previously been involved in criminal activities or the persons' bank accounts or wallets indicate involvement in such.

Prospectus

The Prospectus in almost all jurisdictions serves as **the main document to inform investors about the Offering**. Depending on the jurisdiction, the content and the process of getting approved varies.

Very important as well are the exemptions projects and companies can make use of. If they are utilized, the company may not have to publish a prospectus. This allows projects to collect the first seed capital early on from larger or institutional investors without investing too much effort into setting up the infrastructure and write the prospectus – instead, they can use this time to build the actual product.

---

[3] http://ec.europa.eu/newsroom/just/document.cfm?action=display&doc_id=4893

Regulation of Security Token Offerings (STOs)

Securities law

"Securities law is the field of law that covers transactions and other dealings in securities with the goal of the establishment and maintenance of a fair market for securities to protect investors[4]."

> Depending on the relevant jurisdiction, compliance requirements for securities can constitute legal burdens for token issuers as Bill. It depends on whether the model Bill chooses with its specific characteristics falls under a Regulation such as securities law. Bill now decides to issue shares for equity that do fall under the securities law.

I implicate the applicability of the securities law when speaking about security tokens. Therefore, I will not refer to ICOs in the sense of issuing utility tokens or similar assets that might not fall under securities law.

There are three important subdivisions for token issuers under securities law, constituting duties and restrictions to be followed.

- **Disclosure duties:**
    o Certain information must be made accessible.

- **Restrictions against fraud and manipulation**
    o The issuer has to comply with restrictions against fraud and manipulation.

---

[4] Maas, Thijs – Initital Coin Offerings: When Are tokens Securities in the EU and US?, 2019, p. 26

Regulation of Security Token Offerings (STOs)

- **Restrictions against insider trading**
  o Disclosure obligations of inside information provide further protection of investors from information asymmetries.

Summary

The securities laws sets the requirements for offering securities. the Prospectus, as being one of them, informs investors about the most important facts of the offering.

Central securities depositories (CSDs)

Another element in dealing with securities, are central securities depositories. As the term indicates, such a *depositary* is used as a storage for securities and their transfer. "CSDs operate the infrastructure that enables the so-called securities settlement systems" - this is how a CSD is defined in Europe[5]. Hence, a CSD comes into action when securities are issued (tracking the issuance process), securities are transferred (tracking the ownership) or securities are settled for cash[6].

In order to enable an efficient financial infrastructure e.g. within the European Union, the Central securities depositories Regulation has been implemented as an EU Regulation. Other jurisdictions also make use of regulated CSDs.

---

[5] https://ec.europa.eu/info/business-economy-euro/banking-and-finance/financial-markets/post-trade-services/central-securities-depositories-csds_en

[6] https://ec.europa.eu/info/business-economy-euro/banking-and-finance/financial-markets/post-trade-services/central-securities-depositories-csds_en

Regulation of Security Token Offerings (STOs)

Going back to the roots of Blockchain technologies, the idea of them was to replace intermediaries and eliminate centralized stakeholders. This seems quite contradictory to a CSD - and it is. Since tokens by nature are stored on a Blockchain and mostly also transferred on the Blockchain. Hence, the Blockchain itself might be the CSD: It controls the issuance and settles transactions on the decentralized network. The question about the necessity of a CSD has been raised, Ethereum founder Vitalik Buterin does not see any need for it within a financial system that is built on a distributed ledger[7]. Others claim that a CSD is necessary in order to have a governance body that can control the activities. Whether a CSD is necessary from a technical viewpoint shall not be discussed any further since it reflects the general trade-off between centralization and decentralization like in many other aspects.

Interesting whatsoever is the legal consideration: It has to be determined whether a specific Blockchain platform would be considered as an appropriate CSD by the regulator in order to be compliant with the relevant CSD Regulation e.g. for the European Union. Since this is one of the efficiency gains made possible by utilizing a Blockchain, it is likely that Regulators will adopt certain Blockchains as a valid matter of record-keeping. This, however, is very different at the time-being.

---

[7] https://www.thetradenewscrypto.com/csds-forced-defend-existence-dlt-world/

Specific jurisdictions and Regulations

Within this chapter, a brief overview of the most relevant locations to consider when issuing security tokens shall be given. Everything mentioned above has a general character and is abstracted from a specific jurisdiction. In the following, we will break down the topic further by diving into specific Regulations worldwide.

The selection of the jurisdictions was made A) by the access to available capital within that market B) the level of regulatory advantageousness as well as C) the efforts done by Regulators in order to provide a consistent legal ground for tokenized securities.

Although this chapter shall provide a general view on worldwide Regulations and it was conducted out of months of research of the legal matters, I personally lived and operated in Europe almost my whole life and the focus is slightly shifted towards European jurisdictions. In order to keep the level of detail balanced between the different jurisdictions, you can find further information about the European Regulations online in the readers' portal.

The most popular jurisdictions for a STO
It is a difficult task to find out the most popular location for a STO judging by the number of offerings made since there are only a few examples that can be found for successfully executed ones.

At the same time, the decision about the right jurisdiction for a STO to be executed from shall be based on many different factors and decided on a case-by-case basis. Some jurisdictions have advantageous Regulations towards the public offering of securities or the specific vehicle of security tokens. However, the long-term strategy of a company, it's market and its previous place of incorporation cannot be neglected. Hence, the most popular countries here are also selected by the market impression and intangible knowledge distributed in the heads of thought leaders worldwide that I spoke to in the last years and especially the last six months prior to publishing this book. It does not replace any legal or financial advice from an authorized person.

A) European Union

The European Union as a common economic territory has a financial law that is harmonized to a large degree between the different member states[8]. Therefore, the EU is widely making use of unified Regulations while giving the freedom of choice to member states at certain points. Although the European Union is fragmented into many different countries, this offers possibilities to perform an Offering to many countries without having to go through the whole preparation for every country in order to meet the specific requirements. Europe is known for a rather stable regulatory system and especially the Western countries like Germany for a quite conservative approach towards new technologies. This makes it really interesting for projects to rely on a solid ground for long-term legal stability, but also requires more effort in order to establish a revolutionary breakthrough with new technologies since the laws are less flexible.

The European Securities and Markets Authority (ESMA) is the mainly relevant, independent EU authority dealing with those

---

[8] Maas, Thijs – Initital Coin Offerings: When Are tokens Securities in the EU and US?, 2019

Regulation of Security Token Offerings (STOs)

Regulations. It's purpose is to enhance "the protection of investors and promoting stable and orderly financial markets"[9].

B) Asia

The Asian market is interesting for many projects outside of the region since it is known for holding large resources of capital. Especially the southeast Asian region is relevant in this regard. Within the last years, the tech investments there continuously increased[10]. Asians oftentimes focus on European companies, they seem to like the legal stability in countries like Germany. Statistics prove that the investments from China into Europe are even nine times higher than into North America[11].

Hot spots like Hong Kong provide investment companies a beneficial tax system and regulatory framework. Generally speaking, there is no unified system of law in Asia as it can be found in Europe. Given the fact that most of the capital can be found in a few locations, this might not be necessary.

Asian markets usually resonate the strongest with the adoption of new technology[12] - hence, Asia might not only be a good region as a source for investments, but also an important market to tackle for technical applications.

---

[9] https://www.esma.europa.eu/about-esma/who-we-are
[10] https://www.cento.vc/southeast-asia-tech-investment-2018/
[11] https://www.cnbc.com/2018/07/17/china-is-investing-9-times-more-into-europe-than-into-north-america.html
[12] https://www.gfk.com/en-sg/insights/press-release/asians-show-greater-propensity-amongst-global-consumers-in-new-technology-adoption/

C) United States

The Unites States are known for their open venture capital culture and their risk-friendly approach. Evidence can be found in the latest numbers: The US venture capital investments within 2018 (into US-based startups) reached more than 130 billion US-Dollar and is surpassing the amounts during the Dot Com era[13]. Furthermore, the United States are known for their tech giants and new technology.

Securities are strictly regulated by the Securities and Exchange Commission (SEC). The Regulation however is clearer than in other places and tests that are easy to understand can offer an indication on which Regulation might be applicable.

Regulations within the European Union

In order to give you an understandable overview of the different jurisdictions within the EU, we will first focus on aspects that are unified within the EU and then examine specific differences between relevant member states. This chapter about the EU Regulations goes into detail to a certain extent.

Is the EU a relevant area for STOs?

The EU is known for a quite stable Regulation and as a safe place to operate in. Especially the fact that harmonized Regulation allows to target many countries concurrently without huge additional efforts makes the market interesting for conducting an STO or targeting it. While most of the Regulations are harmonized, some EU countries simplify the process of issuing securities

---

[13] https://nvca.org/pressreleases/us-venture-capital-investment-reached-130-9-billion-2018-surpassing-dot-com-era/

a bit or have faster and more efficient process, allowing the project to put the footstep into the EU and then passport the Prospectus (more details later) in order to target the other EU countries as well.

> Bill wants to operate a digital product startup that is not physically bound to a specific location to operate from. The European market is generally interesting for him and he has a preference for regulatory stability – hence, he wants to incorporate in and conduct the STO out of Europe.

Keep it simple

A *Directive* within the European Union is the specification of a **goal** that has to be achieved by the single member states without exactly dictating them **how**.

A *Regulation* in contrast to that is enforced as law within all the member states.

MiFID

The *Markets in Financial Instruments Directive* (2004/39/EC) is an EU wide Directive that is affecting many activities around financial instruments and financial markets and has been applicable across the European Union since November 2007.

According to ESMA, the MiFID sets out:[14]

---

[14] https://www.esma.europa.eu/policy-rules/mifid-ii-and-mifir

- conduct of business and organizational requirements for investment firms;
- authorization requirements for regulated markets;
- regulatory reporting to avoid market abuse;
- trade transparency obligation for shares; and
- rules on the admission of financial instruments to trading.

MiFID II

A revised version of the original *MiFID* (2004/39/EC) has been adopted by the European Parliament and the Council of the European Union[15], being applicable from 3 January 2018[16]. The revised version is referred to as MiFID II or MiFIR.

The MiFID II is supposed to make markets "fairer, safer and more efficient" [17]. It especially affects investment firms and ensures transparency due to more strict requirements of documentation and reporting. Overall, the aim of MiFID II is to increase the investor protection. The MiFID II is made up out of the *Regulation* (MiFI**R**) and the *Directive* (MiFI**D**). While the rules of the Regulation are applied directly in all Member States, the Directive leaves room for implementation in the Member States.

---

[15] https://www.esma.europa.eu/policy-rules/mifid-ii-and-mifir
[16] https://www.esma.europa.eu/policy-rules/mifid-ii-and-mifir
[17] https://www.esma.europa.eu/policy-rules/mifid-ii-and-mifir

> **Excursus: The details of MiFID**
>
> The following are the most important aspects contained in the MiFID II. Firstly, the Directive strengthens investor protection through, among other things, a definition of independent and dependent advice, a ban on inducements and product governance. Secondly, it contains a provision for market data and data consolidation including a set of rules especially on transparency for Equities in the EU. An important change of MiFID II is the extension of the scope to include non-Equities such as bonds, structured finance products and derivatives. Thirdly, it provides conditions for investment firms on how to authorize and operate. Additionally, it sets out rules for algorithmic and high-frequency trading as well as commodity derivatives. Last but not least, the Directive introduces a new trading venue, the so-called Organized Trading Facility (OTF) as neutral trading platforms, which an investment firm can only become with the permission of the national regulator.
>
> As has been said before, these MiFID rules will have to be implemented by the Member States individually, leaving some room to them on how to do regulate it in practice.
>
> In contrast to that, the rules contained in the MiFIR are applicable directly and therefore are effective consistently across the EU.

Regulation of Security Token Offerings (STOs)

They contain transparency requirements for trading venues, the systematic internalizer business model and trading Over-The-Counter (OTC), including pre-trade as well as post-trade transparency requirements. The MiFIR also requires public disclosure of trades that have been executed as well as transaction reporting to national authorities. Additionally, the MiFIR comprises an obligation for derivatives to be traded on foreseen trading venues (MTF, OTF or the regulated market). Moreover, there is open access to trading venues and central counterparty clearings (CCPs) as well as CCP interoperability. Supervisory authorities receive product intervention powers and there are specific rules for the treatments of entities from third countries operating in the EU.

Keep it simple

To sum it up, the MiFID Directive on the one hand affects activities in financial markets and aims for investor protection while creating a common economic area within the EU. It does so by introducing regulated platforms and rules on trading. The MiFIR Regulation on the other hand contains rules as well as guidelines guaranteeing more transparency in trading activities, introducing requirements on the organization as well as the conduct of actors on the trading markets. It aims at removing trading barriers and providers of clearing services to fuel competition.

Regulation of Security Token Offerings (STOs)

You can find the official ESMA publication under the following link code:

Link Code: 5

Are security Regulations of the EU applicable to security tokens?
The Security Regulation is unlikely to be relevant if the prices of the token are not volatile, the token is not transferable or if the token is backed by e.g. valuables, claims or land, as exclusive assets that cannot be duplicated[18]. Also, all instruments of payment do not fall under security Regulations but under EU banking and payment services Regulation[19]. To be considered as a form of payment requires the possibility of token buyers from day one to buy an actual product or service with it. This requirement might not be fulfilled in many cases.

The applicability of EU security Regulations on security tokens also depends on the specific rights provided by the token.

One of the major questions is: **Does the instrument fall under the term *'transferable security'?*** [20] This is especially relevant for the application of the EU Prospectus Directive or the Prospectus Regulation (more later).

---

[18] Maas, Thijs – Initital Coin Offerings: When Are tokens Securities in the EU and US?, 2019, p. 27
[19] Maas, Thijs – Initital Coin Offerings: When Are tokens Securities in the EU and US?, 2019, p. 52
[20] Maas, Thijs – Initital Coin Offerings: When Are tokens Securities in the EU and US?, 2019, p. 46

The term 'transferable securities' is defined in Art. 4(1)(44) of MIFID II stating that they mean "those classes of securities which are negotiable on the capital market, with the exception of instruments of payment[...]"[21] However, a Directive requires implementation by the Member States and the implementation and interpretation of the term <u>differs</u> between the Member States.

The Member States have implemented the definition of transferable securities in Art. 4(1)(44) MiFID II differently, resulting in differing interpretations in practice[22] [23].

The definition of Art. 4 (1)(44) MIFID II gives some examples for transferable securities, which are explicitly included. In some Member States a certain **degree of equivalence** of a token's design to "shares or other securities equivalent to shares in companies, partnerships or other entities" can mean that this token falls under the Regulation for transferable securities.

The MIFID definition does not prescribe anything about the legal nature of the token issuer and securities in so-called 'other entities' can also fall under the definition. A crucial point is whether a token can be considered to be a security equivalent to shares. This may not be the case if no profit is granted based on

---

[21] https://eur-lex.europa.eu/legal-content/EN/TXT/HTML/?uri=CELEX:32014L0065&from=DE

[22] European Securities and Markets Authority, 'Advice on Initial Coin Offerings and Crypto-Asset, Annex 1: Legal qualification of crypto-assets – survey to NCAs' (ESMA Advice, 9 January 2009) ESMA50-157-1391

[23] Maas, Thijs – Initital Coin Offerings: When Are tokens Securities in the EU and US?, 2019, p. 47

an investment. A factual possibility of return on investment from an increased value of a token is not enough.

The definition provides further categories which fall under the term of 'transferable securities'. Nevertheless, the classification of tokens is not clear, and the equivalence-based approach therefore does not lead to clear results. It became apparent that some Member States have classified tokens under indent (a) of Art. 4(1)(44) MIFID II if economic rights such as revenue or profit rights existed, making tokens equivalent to a share. Others had the additional requirement that the token grants decision-making powers or liquidation rights[24].

Alternatively to the equivalence-based approach, other Member States follow a **characteristics-based** approach to classify tokens. This approach takes into account that Art. 4 (1)(44) MIFID II only contains a non-exhaustive list of possible transferable securities. Other tokens that do not resemble those examples can still fall under the definition without being similar to shares, bonds or one of the other options. Therefore, this approach focuses on the defining characteristics of transferable securities, described in the definition as "classes of securities which are negotiable on the capital market, with the exception of instruments of payment". Three criteria for a transferable security can be derived from this definition: *transferability*, *negotiability* and *standardization*[25].

---

[24] Maas, Thijs – Initital Coin Offerings: When Are tokens Securities in the EU and US?, 2019, p. 47f.

[25] Maas, Thijs – Initital Coin Offerings: When Are tokens Securities in the EU and US?, 2019, p. 49.

Regulation of Security Token Offerings (STOs)

> **Keep it simple**
>
> In order to evaluate whether the issued object classifies under the category of "transferable securities" or not, member states make use of an *equivalence-based* approach or *characteristics-based* approach.

Several Regulations and directives are following under EU securities law that shall not be elaborated within this book to rather give you as a reader a broad overview of the different jurisdictions and make them comparable. Two relevant Regulations and Directives are:

- The Market Abuse Regulation (Council Regulation (EU) No 596/2014 on market abuse OJ L 173)

The Regulation shall combat insider trading and market manipulation. It determines what actions are legal or illegal and is legally binding in all Member States

- The MIFID II (Council Directive 2014/65/EU on markets in financial instruments OJ L 173) shall further strengthen the protection of investors and improve operability of financial markets, increasing efficiency, resilience and transparency. Overall it aims to make the EU more competitive by creating a single market for investment services and activities while ensuring harmonized investor protection[26].

---

[26] https://www.esma.europa.eu/policy-rules/mifid-ii-and-mifir

Regulation of Security Token Offerings (STOs)

> As Bill already decided, he wants to give out shares of the company in return for investments. These should be tradable on an exchange and are expected to have a fluctuating price. He gets to know that the issued shares fall under the term "transferable securities". Apart from that, Bill and his team have begun writing the Whitepaper that should inform customers and investors about the project and their Fundraising efforts.

Prospectus

The prospectus is one of most important artifacts involved into a public offering of securities. The aim is to inform investors about the terms and conditions of an offer. In order to that, the EU Regulations specify the necessity of a prospectus and the information it must contain.

A Public offering of "transferable securities" in the EU requires a prospectus, which has to be approved by the national financial regulator of an EU Member State[27].

Currently, member states possess a greater ability to define certain requirements regarding the prospectus. The *Prospectus Directive* that is effective by the time this book is being written sets boundaries and ranges in which the member states can implement their specific requirements.

However, the *New Prospectus Regulation* will come into force by 21st of July in 2019. From that point on, the member states have

---

[27] https://thetokenist.io/how-2019-will-see-new-legislation-to-favor-european-based-security-token-offerings/

less freedom in implementing the requirements due to the harmonization this Regulation is aiming for. In the following, we will compare both, however, focus on the future New Prospectus Regulation.

A) *The Prospectus Directive*

On the prospectus to be published when securities are offered to the public or admitted to trading, amended by **Council Directive 2010/73/EU** on the prospectus to be published when securities are offered to the public or admitted to trading.

Since this is a Directive, the EU member states possess the freedom of designing the implementation and could have a different treatment of securities offerings. This is the case for limits of the raised money that, when exceeded, would require a prospectus. It can be set between one and eight million Euros.

The new Regulation with further harmonization will come into effect in 2019:

B) *The New Prospectus Regulation* [28] (will come into force on 21st of July 2019)

On the prospectus to be published when securities are offered to the public or admitted to trading on a regulated market.

The content of a prospectus[29]

There is certain information required by law that a prospectus has to contain. From 21st of July onwards those will be regulated according Art. 6 REGULATION (EU) 2017/1129.

---

[28] https://ec.europa.eu/info/law/prospectus-Regulation-eu-2017-1129_en
[29] https://ec.europa.eu/info/law/prospectus-Regulation-eu-2017-1129_en-

Regulation of Security Token Offerings (STOs)

The minimum information required by law is:

"information which is material to an investor for making an informed assessment of
(a) the assets and liabilities, profits and losses, financial position, prospects of the issues and of any guarantor;
(b) the rights attaching to the securities; and
(c) the reasons for the issuance and its impact on the issues."

A prospectus therefore e.g. includes the amount of money that shall be raised, the investment ticket size, type of investors addressed, location of investors, public or private sale.

Further requirements to its content are:
- The information has to be understandable
- No contradictory statements

> **Keep it simple**
> The prospectus is the main offering document and the Prospectus Directive sets the requirements for the content that needs to be contained. From 21st of July 2019, the new Prospectus Regulation will come into force and be responsible for that.

Is the Whitepaper a prospectus?

Especially ICOs in the early times were publishing a whitepaper as the main document for token buyers of their offering. This however does not replace a prospectus. Considering the *whitepaper* term as it is known within the space of Blockchain startups and ICOs is therefore not comparable to an official prospectus. The need for

Regulation of Security Token Offerings (STOs)

an approval by an authority already implicates that most of the published whitepapers in the past did not meet the requirements of a prospectus.

Looking at the facts the other way around, a prospectus eliminates the need of writing a whitepaper, because it also aims to inform investors but is not legally binding[30].

> Bill and his team have already written the whitepaper but noticed that the Prospectus has a defined content to be included by law. Hence, they keep the whitepaper as a summary of their vision and their plan for the next years and create a new document for the Prospectus. Most of the information can be adapted and a few details have to be added to clearly show the investor what he might be investing into and how the financial product is constructed. Bill is a bit frustrated since writing the prospectus, doublechecking and proofreading it, getting a legal opinion, handing it in to the respective authority and then awaiting the approval would take at least a couple of weeks. He asks his lawyer if there is a possibility to avoid the need of writing a prospectus. Indeed...

---

[30] https://blog.neufund.org/demystifying-the-prospectus-part-1-1e3d3fec8d98

Exemptions

There are certain exemptions in which a prospectus is not needed[31]. Making use of the exemption includes the following requirements.

- **Qualified investors exemption/ private placement**
  The tokens are only sold to *qualified investors* and high net worth individuals (HNWI) as defined by the law[32]

- **"limited offer" exemption for STOs**
  Less than a specific amount, depending on the member state, is raised. The threshold can be chosen by the member state within a range of EUR 1 000 000 and EUR 8 000 000)[33]. When the new Prospectus Regulation comes into force, there will be a unified, EU wide threshold set.

- **If the tokens are offered to a maximum of 149 people**

- **"nominal value" exemption**
  The price of each unit is at least 100,000 Euro

- **"large investments" exemption**
  Each investor buys a minimum of e.g. 100,000 Euro worth of the token

---

[31] https://cryptovest.com/education/guide-to-legalities-of-security-token-offerings-stos-the-road-less-travelled/
[32] https://cryptovest.com/education/guide-to-legalities-of-security-token-offerings-stos-the-road-less-travelled/
[33] http://www.kinanis.com/security-token-offerings-sto

Regulation of Security Token Offerings (STOs)

> **Keep it simple**
> When the project makes use of exemptions, it can proceed without fulfilling the requirement for a prospectus.

Bill and his team are launching a digital product that targets the same people that also would invest into STOs. Hence, their purpose of conducting a STO also is to include many investors that afterwards want to use their services and stay in as long-term investors. However, they anyway need a long time to finalize the product and now want to focus on that instead of handling large numbers of investors. Hence, they decide to concentrate on a few, larger investors within the first step and then include smaller investors later. This allows them to focus on actually building the product and also might eliminate the need for a prospectus to be written since they would only target a small group of investors with larger stakes they are buying.

Licensing requirements

Further Licensing requirements (beside compliance with the securities law) apply:

Tokens which are not considered to fall under securities law, can still be considered as e-money, a payment service or as an alternative investment, which is why other licenses might be

Regulation of Security Token Offerings (STOs)

required, depending on the relevant jurisdiction (which is again depending on the origin of the clients)[34]

- The legal relationship between the token issuer and buyer can lead to a distinction between unregulated payment token and e-money or a payment service
- If issuer has the liability e.g. to buy back the coin, usually a license is required[35]

Generally speaking, an issuer does not require a license to offer a security token, if the prospectus he has drafted is approved by the responsible securities regulator[36].

What are the differences between EU Member states?
In the following, the most relevant EU countries that offer special regulatory advantages will be discussed in detail. The aim is to give a broad overview of the different countries and their approaches - still, the content is very simplified and further research shall be made to decide for a specific jurisdiction to operate in or from.

STOs within the European Union

Regulations in Cyprus
Cyprus is a location that is often being discussed in regard to cryptocurrency and ICO Regulations. However, looking at the facts

---

[34] https://cryptovest.com/education/guide-to-legalities-of-security-token-offerings-stos-the-road-less-travelled/
[35] https://cryptovest.com/education/guide-to-legalities-of-security-token-offerings-stos-the-road-less-travelled/
[36] https://cryptovest.com/education/guide-to-legalities-of-security-token-offerings-stos-the-road-less-travelled/

Regulation of Security Token Offerings (STOs)

for STOs, Cyprus does not seem to have a competitive advantage against other EU jurisdictions.

The Prospectus exemption amount of raised capital is set at one million Euro for Cyprus, the lowest end. Exceeding it would require a Prospectus. Hence, the threshold is much lower than in other EU countries such as Malta, Lithuania, Italy or Germany[37].

Similar to Malta, Cyprus offers advantageous tax structures compared to other EU countries. The corporate tax equals 12,5 percent[38].

Regulations in Germany

Germany is known for their strong and traditional economy as well as for their conservative Regulations. The Federal Financial Supervisory Authority (BaFin) is responsible for regulating securities and other offerings and the institution the Prospectus has to be handed in to in order to obtain an approval.

The BaFin states:

> "Securities and other investment products may not be offered for sale to the public in Germany without a prospectus; and the publication of any such prospectus requires the prior permission of BaFin[39]."

---

[37] http://www.mondaq.com/cyprus/x/760180/Securities/Security+Token+Offerings+STOs+The+Future+of+Coin+Offerings
[38] https://flagtheory.com/securities-token-exchange/
[39] https://www.bafin.de/EN/Aufsicht/Prospekte/prospekte_node_en.html

Although Germany is known for a quite conservative approach towards allowing new technologies, the BaFin increasingly recognized the topic by releasing several publications dealing with that topic and ramping up their capacity for this area. At the same time, they approved the first projects to operate in the field of security tokens. This sets a positive expectation for the German market to be a targeted market of investors. However, awaiting the approvals and time-consuming processes might not make Germany to one of the top jurisdictions to incorporate the STO conducting company in, depending on the operations.

Regulations in Gibraltar

Gibraltar is known as a jurisdiction where many insurance, gaming and financial companies are registered in and promises an advantageous tax system[40]. The landscape of exchanges, which is mostly concentrated on two divisions, has been covering both ICOs and STOs early on. The Gibraltar Blockchain Exchange (GBX) is the national exchange to list utility tokens and cryptocurrencies while the Gibraltar Stock Exchange (GSX) focuses on securities. The GSX announced in April 2019 that they started listing tokenized securities and hence is one of the first exchanges worldwide to do so[41]. Since secondary markets are one of the elements of the security token infrastructure, this sets Gibraltar apart from many other places where competitors are awaiting their approvals and licenses.

---

[40] https://www.gibraltarfinance.gi/en/home
[41] https://www.gsx.gi/article/9466/the-gibraltar-stock-exchange-set-to-offer-digital-debt-securities-and-funds

Depending on the Brexit decisions, things can get a bit more complicated when dealing with Gibraltar, although it should still have an access both to the British market as well as to the European Economic Area (EEA). The difference to locations like Malta is the argument that decision makers and the physical operations are usually based elsewhere, hence a real Blockchain ecosystem on Gibraltar can hardly be found[42].

Regulations in Netherlands
Netherlands has a long history in the field of Finance since Amsterdam was the first place to have a stock exchange worldwide[43]. The jurisdiction is especially relevant since it combines a financially strong country with regulatory advantages: The threshold for a Prospectus requirement is set to five million Euro, similar to other countries[44]. If less than five million Euro is raised within 12 months, the requirements are comparably low. So, the Netherlands are especially relevant for projects raising up to five million Euro and focusing on national investments.

Certain structures within the Netherlands allow an advantageous separation of voting and dividend rights.

Regulations in Liechtenstein (European Economic Area)
Liechtenstein is a very small country within the heart of Europe. That allows the country to act dynamically on technological

---

[42] https://www.ico.li/the-search-for-blockchain-island/
[43] https://hackernoon.com/on-worlds-security-token-offering-epicenter-the-netherlands-1561938cf1eb
[44] https://www.esma.europa.eu/sites/default/files/library/esma31-62-1193_prospectus_thresholds.pdf

advancements and requirements, but grants access to the European market because it is part of the European Economic Area (EEA)[45]. It is not part of the EU though[46]. Especially interesting is that Liechtenstein "enjoy[s] excellent, friendly relations with traditionally close ties"[47] as well and hence has a good access to two highly relevant territories with a significant capital: both the EU and Switzerland.

With the own Liechtenstein *Blockchain Act*, the principality wants to pave the way for tokenizing assets in many different ways. Therefore, *the* token is "introduced as a new legal element in Liechtenstein law"[48].

A token, according to this Act, is not specifically defined in order to represent a specific type of asset. Instead, a *Token Container* model is implemented. This model expresses that a token is a "Representation of Right on [a] Blockchain-System"[49]. This means the container can be filled with different rights, like the examples of a governments' presentation about the Act reveals:
- security token would mean the container is filled with a security

---

[45] https://www.liechtenstein.li/en/country-and-people/state/form-of-government-and-constitution/
[46] https://www.welt.de/wirtschaft/article176522498/Liechtenstein-EU-Beitritt-ist-kein-Thema.html
[47] https://www.eda.admin.ch/eda/en/home/representations-and-travel-advice/liechtenstein/switzerland-liechtenstein.html
[48] http://www.ecri.eu/system/tdf/thomas_duenser_1.pdf?file=1&type=node&id=155&force=0 p. 14
[49] http://www.ecri.eu/system/tdf/thomas_duenser_1.pdf?file=1&type=node&id=155&force=0 p. 14

- A utility coin contrarily is a container that is filled with a software usage right

More important are the legal consequences resulting out of the classification / the application. Speaking about a security token, this would mean that the Security Laws and Financial Market Laws are applicable[50]. So, Liechtenstein is approaching the subject in a technical matter first by saying that if an asset exists in the form of a token, it shall be considered according to the *Token Container*. Then, the legal and regulatory considerations are taken into account and the consequences subsequently upon the classification of the underlying asset.

The relation between the actual right and the tokenized representation can be classified by using this approach. For example, the consequences of a token transfer and the legal status of the owner and possessor of a token can be outlined.

Regulations in Switzerland
Switzerland has a long history of welcoming companies from the financial industry and a mixed reputation along with it. Low taxes and business-friendly Regulations are the reason for many to choose Switzerland as the place to go to[51]. Switzerland is neither a member of the EU, nor of the EEA[52].

---

[50] http://www.ecri.eu/system/tdf/thomas_duenser_1.pdf?file=1&type=node&id=155&force=0 p. 15
[51] https://dailyhodl.com/2018/12/25/legal-aspects-of-sto-in-switzerland-how-to-issue-security-tokens-in-crypto-valley/
[52] https://www.gov.uk/eu-eea

Regulation of Security Token Offerings (STOs)

Switzerland was the first country to issue a guidance on ICOs in 2018 with the Swiss Financial Markets Supervisory Authority (FINMA)[53]. Generally speaking, the country established itself as a mayor crypto nation within Europe, especially with the region of Zug till the point it got named the *Crypto Valley*[54].

The FINMA distinguishes tokens into three different categories: *payment tokens*, *utility tokens* and *asset tokens* or hybrids of them[55]. For the purpose we are following in this book, asset tokens are most likely the case to deal with. Asset tokens are treated like securities - the FINMA "regards asset tokens as securities"- meaning that the usual securities law requirements for trading them and civil law requirements apply[56].

Switzerland has a five often relevant regulatory elements for primary markets that are being refered to as the Big5:
(i) Stock Exchange Regulation
(ii) Anti Money Laundering Regulation
(iii) Banking Regulation
(iv) Financial Market Infrastructure Regulation
(v) Collective Investment Scheme Regulation[57]

---

[53] https://medium.com/mme-legal/securities-token-offerings-stos-in-switzerland-3ad2e6ec5718
[54] https://dailyhodl.com/2018/12/25/legal-aspects-of-sto-in-switzerland-how-to-issue-security-tokens-in-crypto-valley/
[55] https://www.finma.ch/en/news/2018/02/20180216-mm-ico-wegleitung/
[56] https://www.finma.ch/en/news/2018/02/20180216-mm-ico-wegleitung/
[57] https://medium.com/mme-legal/securities-token-offerings-stos-in-switzerland-3ad2e6ec5718

Regulation of Security Token Offerings (STOs)

STOs in Asia
Regulation in Hong Kong
Hong Kong is referred to as "the world's 'freest economy'" in regard to their low tax rates, free trade and a very little interference of the government. Unlike the belief of many people, Hong Kong is a Special Administrative Region and quite independent from the mainland China.

Due to the economic advantages such as low tax rates, Hong Kong mostly consists of companies within the service sector and incorporates many financial activities. It is also seen as an easier gateway to access the Chinese market than approaching the Chinese mainland directly. At the same time, the Hong Kong Stock Exchange is very popular for companies from the mainland China that prefer a more open environment[58].

Securities and Futures Commission (SFC) released a special statement on STOs in March 2019. It defines them as "specific offerings which are structured to have features of traditional securities offerings and involve Security Token[...]". According to the SFC, security tokens are likely to be considered as securities under the Securities and Futures Ordinance (SFO). In this case, the securities laws would be applicable[59]. While the economic environment of Hong Kong offers a lot of capital to be invested, people claim that Hong Kong makes STOs to a privilege for the

---

[58] https://www.investopedia.com/articles/investing/121814/hong-kong-vs-china-understand-differences.asp
[59] https://www.sfc.hk/web/EN/news-and-announcements/policy-statements-and-announcements/statement-on-security-token-offerings.html

Regulation of Security Token Offerings (STOs)

"super rich" to invest in since only institutional investors that have a portfolio of at least one million US-Dollar are allowed to do so[60].

Especially relevant for foreign STOs is that they shall be licensed in order to market their offer to Hong Kong based investors[61].

Overall, Hong Kong offers a friendly environment to new technological developments within the financial sector, also express with the Fintech Supervisory Sandbox (FSS)[62].

Regulation in Singapore

Singapore is known for a quite friendly attitude towards Blockchain technologies - not only the launch of a regulatory sandbox by the Monetary Authority indicates that innovation is tackled on the government level[63]. They even released "A Guide to Digital Token Offerings"[64].

As long as digital tokens are classified as capital markets products in Singapore, they shall be regulated under the Securities and Futures Act (SFA).

---

[60] https://bitcoinist.com/hong-kong-sfc-sto-investing/#SFC_Not_an_Outright_Ban_But_Almost_as_Bad

[61] https://bitcoinist.com/hong-kong-sfc-sto-investing/#SFC_Not_an_Outright_Ban_But_Almost_as_Bad

[62] https://www.hkma.gov.hk/eng/key-functions/international-financial-centre/fintech-supervisory-sandbox.shtml

[63] https://stonetwork.com/Regulation/singapore-security-token-offering-Regulation/

[64] http://www.mas.gov.sg/~/media/MAS/News%20and%20Publications/Monographs%20and%20Information%20Papers/Guide%20to%20Digital%20Token%20Offerings%20last%20updated%20on%2030%20Nov.pdf

Regulation of Security Token Offerings (STOs)

When certain criteria, such as being classified as a small (personal) offer, the execution as a private placement and the approach to solely institutional and accredited investors, is met, there shall be an exemption from the Prospectus Requirements.

The fact that the Authorities not only cover the Regulation of the asset itself, but also define certain stakeholders such as the trading platform and their roles, is very helpful.

The environment in Singapore for security tokens is overall far ahead of many other Asian regions since the government enhances such technologies by providing fast regulatory responses, an established financial ecosystem and concrete regulatory guidance.

Regulation in China

According to Representatives of Beijing's Municipal Bureau of Finance, STO fund-raising activities are illegal in Beijing[65]. Hence, conducting an STO within the mainland of China does not seem a viable option. Evidence for the distant approach of the government towards those topics could already be found back in 2017 when ICOs were banned[66].

---

[65] https://www.coindesk.com/security-token-offerings-illegal-says-beijing-financial-watchdog
[66] https://www.coindesk.com/chinas-ico-ban-a-full-translation-of-regulator-remarks

Regulation of Security Token Offerings (STOs)

Regulation in Japan

Japan is aiming for a high investor protection with specific actions taken in the last years. The Regulator is however open to Blockchain based assets and is generally known for being crypto-friendly[67].

When a token falls under the type of securities, it shall be monitored by the Financial Instruments and Exchange Act (FIEA), not falling under crypto asset Regulations[68]. The protective approach Japan takes in specific areas, such as the requirement for securities firms to separate customers' and companies' assets into different accounts[69], strengthens the reputation of the Japanese regulator.

Overall, Japan at the first sight looks like an environment with clear Regulation, a friendly approach towards new technologies and a place with high protection for investors.

Regulation in Thailand

Thailand experienced an increase of corporate venture capital (CVC) investments within the last years and the government was especially strengthening the VC culture by providing advantageous tax treatments in 2018[70]. Looking at the numbers, the

---

[67] https://www.cryptoinvestor.asia/japans-financial-regulator-mulls-security-token-regime-for-cryptocurrencies/
[68] https://thetokenist.io/japans-primary-financial-regulatory-seeks-to-amend-its-cryptocurrency-related-business-law/
[69] https://www.cryptoinvestor.asia/japans-financial-regulator-mulls-security-token-regime-for-cryptocurrencies/
[70] https://www.lexology.com/library/detail.aspx?g=eb75508f-6076-4025-bf4c-8c63a2b7f2fa

investments from Thailand are however small compared to other Asian regions[71].

While the venture capital industry is making progress on the first sight, the Regulation for STOs is quite unclear. The decision makers explicitly say that they have not decided "whether STOs fall under the SEC Act or the Digital Asset Act, but it depends on the STO's conditions and the details in its white paper"[72].

Hence, Thailand is changing from a regulatory perspective, whatsoever is a comparingly small market in Asia to obtain investment capital from.

Regulation in Russia

People often presume that Russia is inhabited by many rich individuals. Indeed, Russia being called "one of the most unequal places on Earth"[73], does have a network of high net worth individuals that are actively investing.

After Russians played a big role in the ICO hype within 2017, they stepped a bit back afterwards and some projects turned out not to be successful, leading to the fact that the Forbes Magazine expressed that "Russians seem to be the ones affiliated with

---

[71] https://www.thailand-business-news.com/tech/71058-thailand-tech-startup-ecosystem-report-2018.html
[72] https://www.bangkokpost.com/business/news/1584098/regulators-stymied-by-sto-peculiarities
[73] https://meduza.io/en/feature/2019/01/23/the-top-1-controls-a-third-of-the-wealth-and-the-poor-are-getting-poorer-how-russia-became-one-of-the-most-unequal-places-on-earth

Regulation of Security Token Offerings (STOs)

crypto fraud"[74]. The Waves platform[75], as a Russian startup, is a well-known project in the industry that seemed to be in contact with the securities regulators during 2017 in order to build a joint blockchain platform.

Since then, only little progress in the Regulation of digital assets can be seen[76].

Very recent news from the earlier months in 2019 however indicate that things are supposed to change: Vladimir Putin should have required the government to draft blockchain and crypto Regulations till July 1, 2019[77]. Furthermore, the new bill "On Digital Financial Assets" has been released that was hoped to enlighten the regulatory sphere on digital assets in Russia - experts are however doubting that this will enable the region to become an interesting jurisdiction for STOs[78].

---

[74] https://www.forbes.com/sites/kenrapoza/2019/01/02/will-russia-make-any-waves-in-crypto-this-year/
[75] https://wavesplatform.com
[76] https://www.forbes.com/sites/kenrapoza/2019/01/02/will-russia-make-any-waves-in-crypto-this-year/
[77] https://coinidol.com/crypto-Regulations-russia/
[78] https://decenter.org/en/analyzing-the-russian-law-on-digital-financial-assets

Regulation in South America

South America and especially the Latin American part is still characterized by a large population of unbanked people[79]. On the one hand, this might let it look like an uninteresting market. On the other hand, especially Blockchain technologies can solve these issues surrounding millions of people due to the lack of bank access[80] and the preliminary requirements such as a solid Identity management solution. Fresh IT companies utilizing decentralized technologies could soften the tense situation while taking into account the loss of credibility that some presidents faced. The population, consequently, is more open to alternative investments. While some positive signs indicate the recognition of crypto assets and security tokens, such as the launch of a security token by the biggest Latin American bank, South America generally lacks a unified Regulation[81] that can be found within the European Union for example.

An advantage of South American countries is the fact that they are more familiar with cryptocurrencies than many other countries. Especially the bad financial infrastructure and access to banks for individuals in Argentina[82], as well as the political and

---

[79] https://blog.neufund.org/a-glance-at-the-state-of-blockchain-in-latin-america-aac3ce148c04

[80] https://blog.neufund.org/a-glance-at-the-state-of-blockchain-in-latin-america-aac3ce148c04

[81] https://www.ampliv.io/sto-checklist-what-you-need-to-know-about-sto-Regulations-in-south-america/

[82] https://www.coindesk.com/crypto-startups-in-argentina-inflation-bitcoin

economic instability within Venezuela[83] made many people to shift their wealth into cryptocurrencies. Supposedly, understanding the process of an STO would be much easier for them and they find it easier to invest.

Since South America does not seem like a very interesting regulatory sphere to operate in or from, the specifics of the most relevant countries will only be covered briefly.

Brazil
The biggest investment bank in South America, has announced to launch a security token that is backed by real estate in Brazil[84]. This is a really positive signal since established players are putting their name tag on tokenized securities.

Chile
Chile seems to consider cryptocurrencies, but also crowdfunding purposes related to Blockchain in the bills they are drafting. Since the Ministry of Energy planned to utilize the Ethereum Blockchain for tracking and recording data, the governments in Chile are valuing the potential of it[85].

Mexico
Mexico has an existing environment of startups and fintechs. The approved "Ley fintech" law makes the Regulation very clear

---

[83] https://bitcoinist.com/venezuela-60-million-bitcoin-2019/
[84] https://thetokenist.io/latin-americas-largest-investment-bank-will-launch-its-own-security-token/
[85] http://energiaabierta.cl

Regulation of Security Token Offerings (STOs)

and also very concrete by focusing on crypto companies, crowd-fundings and APIs. A sandbox strengthens those efforts[86].

---

[86] https://blog.neufund.org/a-glance-at-the-state-of-blockchain-in-latin-america-aac3ce148c04

Regulation of Security Token Offerings (STOs)

Urugay

Similar to Chile, Urugay lacks concrete Regulations but has formed a government committee in order to develop a bill that covers crypto assets and Blockchain related businesses[87].

South American countries with unclear or prohibitive Regulations

The Regulation is quite unclear or even prohibitive in the following South American countries: Bolivia, Cuba, Ecuador, El Salvador, Guatemala, Honduras, Nicaragua, Peru, Dominican Republic[88].

Regulations in the United States

The United States have a special role in the context of token offerings: They were the region that most often got excluded from ICOs during the hype in 2017 and 2018. Almost every project that was raising money through an ICO was asking the investors to confirm they are not a US person or resident[89]. They were fearing the consequences in the case that their efforts would be classified as a securities' offering that they were not fulfilling the requirements for. Hogan Lovells (one of the biggest law firms of the world) at one point recommended to not offer tokensales to Americans[90].

---

[87] https://blog.neufund.org/a-glance-at-the-state-of-blockchain-in-latin-america-aac3ce148c04
[88] https://blog.neufund.org/a-glance-at-the-state-of-blockchain-in-latin-america-aac3ce148c04
[89] https://www.coininsider.com/why-arent-certain-icos-open-to-us-citizens/
[90] https://news.bitcoin.com/some-icos-now-ban-americans-who-should-expect-more-ostracism/

Regulation of Security Token Offerings (STOs)

The **Howey Test** (explained below) is still relevant when deciding if a transaction represents an investment contract. If this is the case, many regulatory requirements apply. Oftentimes, projects try to avoid being classified as such.

This does not mean at all the United States are not a relevant market. Rather, projects back in times were able to raise enough money outside the US and hence did not want to take the unnecessary risk of entering that market.

Speaking of STOs, they would by nature classify as a security and need to follow the Regulations or make use of exemptions. The region is still known as the "home for venture capital" - the overall amount of Asian and US venture capital investments remains at a similar level[91]. Hence, it also remains one of the most relevant jurisdictions.

The Howey Test
As depicted above, the Howey test aims to classify transactions as securities or not.

There is the story of a citrus farm back in 1946. People were buying the land with a profit expectation from the citrus farm that was run by the Howey Company on that land. The SEC did not allow this sale to happen because of the profit expectation associated with it - and marked an important step in the definition of securities.

---

[91] https://www.ft.com/content/ccd356f6-f67d-11e7-88f7-5465a6ce1a00

Regulation of Security Token Offerings (STOs)

A transaction is classified as a security when all of the four criteria are met:
1. There is an investment of money
2. There is an expectation of profits
3. The investment of money is in a common enterprise
4. Any profit comes from the efforts of a promoter or third party"[92]

Coming back to the example and checking the criteria with the facts, it is very obvious that the transaction of the citrus farm land would be classified as a security.

Relevant Regulations within the United States

The Securities Act
The Securities Act was invented to protect investors. It aims for two goals:
- Transparency to inform investors
- Preventing fraud and misrepresentation in the market of securities

Projects hence have to register with the Securities and Exchange Commission (SEC).

---

[92] https://www.coinist.io/the-howey-test-the-sec-and-ico/

Regulation of Security Token Offerings (STOs)

Exemptions

There are three distinct exemptions projects can make use of in order to simplify the process and fall under advantageous regulatory treatments[93].

The three exemptions Reg D, Reg A+ and Reg CF are distinct[94].

Reg D

Reg D consists of three different rules to follow that will not be discussed in detail here. A general solicitation of the Fundraising is possible when certain conditions are met. The restriction on reselling the security is a disadvantage of Reg D[95].

Reg A+

Reg A+ is generally more relevant for established businesses for two years of financial statements are required. A huge advantage compared to Reg D is that there is no restriction on reselling the security[96]. The Reg A+ is interesting when less than 50 million US-Dollar should be raised, and it is wished to approach non-accredited investors as well.

This is why the Reg A+ exemption is highly relevant for STOs.

---

[93] https://icodog.io/security-tokens/overview-of-us-Regulations-of-security-token-offerings/
[94] https://icodog.io/security-tokens/overview-of-us-Regulations-of-security-token-offerings/
[95] https://icodog.io/security-tokens/overview-of-us-Regulations-of-security-token-offerings/
[96] https://icodog.io/security-tokens/overview-of-us-Regulations-of-security-token-offerings/

Reg CF
Reg CF allows to raise up to 1.07 million US-Dollar and is rather interesting for early-stage startups or smaller project. The simpler process however comes with a 12-month lock in which the tokens cannot be resold[97].

Regulation in Australia
Australia is a generally well-developed region[98] that people would most probably expect to find a solid investment culture in. While the human development is at a high standard, experts are raising awareness for the complex structure of financial Regulations[99]. The Regulator states that "a financial product that references or is linked to cryptoassets is subject to the standard regulatory regime under the Corporations Act that applies to that kind of specific product"[100]. By doing so, the Australian Securities and Investments Commission (ASIC) enables experts from the financial field to adopt their experience with financial Regulations for security tokens on the one hand. On the other hand, this might cause some difficulties when token specifics that cannot be compared to the concept of classical financial products are tackled. Such Offerings could require a Prospectus to be published according to the

---

[97] https://icodog.io/security-tokens/overview-of-us-Regulations-of-security-token-offerings/
[98] http://hdr.undp.org/en/countries/profiles/AUS
[99] https://www.theaustralian.com.au/australia-has-a-problem-with-investment-culture-that-must-be-addressed/news-story/1cc76c6c18055af05585c60dae7111a5
[100] https://asic.gov.au/regulatory-resources/digital-transformation/initial-coin-offerings-and-crypto-currency

respective requirements. Judging by the attitude towards cryptocurrencies, the ASIC has shown a rather controversial opinion on them, issuing warnings in regard to unregulated fields[101].

It is believed that classifications into a security token, investment token, payment token, currency token, and a utility token shall be done. Security tokens are defined as following in a publication from the Australian Regulators:

"'Security tokens confer the right of payment against an issuer, either on a corporate basis like dividends or on a contractual basis like repayment of principal/interest under the loan.'" [102]

This might also result in the requirement of a special license.

---

[101] https://www.moneysmart.gov.au/investing/investment-warnings/virtual-currencies

[102] https://medium.com/@nevenka_58628/australian-financial-market-creates-new-rules-for-security-tokens-5139ab363278

Regulation of Security Token Offerings (STOs)

Summary of STO Regulations

When you are not a lawyer or you have not dealt with many legal decisions in the past, this chapter was probably a bit more difficult for you to read. So, what is the essence you should take away, especially if you are not a lawyer:

1. Selling securities is regulated almost everywhere and brings up certain licensing requirements, necessary approvals and boundaries.

2. Both the jurisdiction the company is incorporated in, as well as the jurisdictions to which the securities are sold to, have to be considered.

3. The Prospectus serves as the main Offering document in most of the jurisdictions and has to follow requirements of specific content to be included.

4. Depending on the type of investors that are targeted (e.g. professional investors vs. retail investors) different requirement levels or investor protection measures apply.

5. Many jurisdictions treat security tokens similar to any other security, meaning that the token is just a matter of keeping ownership records of those assets.

6. The Regulators are just starting to react to security tokens, which still remain a new invention. Hence, regulatory considerations may change frequently.

Regulation of Security Token Offerings (STOs)

Book Summary

Tokenization means creating digital assets that allow for interoperability, liquidity and global scaling. It enables many asset classes to become liquid the first time in history such as art when it can be bought in fractions. While liberating the market of assets that only a small part of the population has access to, the issuance of tokenized assets also gets more efficient. Compared to an IPO, the issuance of tokenized shares is possible without many of the previously needed intermediaries and certain parts are outsourced to the Blockchain – the clearing and settlement is no longer an obligation of the banks and makes the market much more efficient.

Considering all the positive aspects of Blockchain technologies, the tokenization of assets and Security Token Offerings, the regulatory sphere is unclear at the time of writing. Certain jurisdictions moved forward and explicitly pushed considerations of tokenized assets forward. Hence, a time with many groundbreaking changes and reactions from governments and authorities can be expected within the next months and years.

I am personally convinced that tokens will replace the existing infrastructure and financial ecosystem – eventually including many of the same stakeholders. However, it is just a matter of time until they will outperform classically issued shares.

Closing words

Thank you for reading Assets on Blockchain. The purpose of this book is to convey the state-of-the art of tokenization and Security Token Offerings. As you may guess, the path does not end here.

First of all, you are invited to join the Assets On Blockchain community with the code at the end of this page. You will find additional information, references and updates there that you will receive with our newsletter.

To keep in touch, you can follow Assets on Blockchain through social media channels and also connect with fellow readers to exchange thoughts and knowledge and grow together. We have created a LinkedIn think tank as well as a Telegram channel. Both can be found in the book lounge.

I personally want to wish you all the best and hope to stay in touch with you.

Max

maxkops.com

Closing words

Important Links
- The official website: **AssetsOnBlockchain.com**

- onsulting session application page: **AssetsOnBlockchain.com/session**

- More about our accelerator program: **AssetsOnBlockchain.com/Accelerator**

The exclusive readers' portal

The portal is available at: assetsonblockchain.com/booklounge

Login code: **20aob19**

The appendix can be found under the link code X"

Apply for a free Consulting session

Since my partners and I got approached a lot for acceleration and coaching projects to help Blockchain Startups and STOs, we decided to launch a free Consulting session program. In this quick, 15 minutes session, we will answer your most important questions in the realm of tokenization, Blockchain based assets and Security Token Offerings (STOs).

Since we are only able to proceed with a limited number of projects, we have to preselect them. You can apply at assetsonblockchain.com/session by submitting your project information and you will receive an answer within two weeks whether the Max Kops & Assets on Blockchain team can offer you the free Consulting session to bring your project to the next level.

There is no obligation, no contract and no fee for you. We just like to offer the sessions to give something back to our readers and members of our Accelerator. Hence, we will treat the few selected projects like our members of the Accelerator and help with the knowledge, network, and publicity we have instead of doing a sales pitch.

Imprint

Responsible person: Maximilian Lukas Kops
Blockerix OÜ (register code: 14611747)
Sepapaja tn 6
15551 Tallinn
Estonia

contact@blockerix.com

Printed in Poland
by Amazon Fulfillment
Poland Sp. z o.o., Wrocław